The Food, the Bad, and the Ugly

by

Frank Cassano

illustrated by

Alastair Duncan

The Food, the Bad, and the Ugly

NOTE: This book is intended purely for entertainment purposes only. All of the material in this book is intended for purposes of SATIRE, PARODY, and HUMOR. None of the views expressed in this book should be confused with the actual views of the author or the publisher.

For information about special discounts for bulk purchases, please contact Sunbury Press, Inc. Wholesale Dept. at (717) 254-7274 or orders@sunburypress.com.

To request one of our authors for speaking engagements or book signings, please contact Sunbury Press, Inc. Publicity Dept. at publicity@sunburypress.com.

FIRST SUNBURY PRESS EDITION
Printed in the United States of America
April 2011

ISBN 978-1-934597-40-8

Published by:
Sunbury Press
Camp Hill, PA
www.sunburypress.com

Camp Hill, Pennsylvania USA

Dedication

This book is dedicated to my parents.

And to people who like to laugh at their food.

Acknowledgments

My heartfelt gratitude goes out to Mark Dawidziak -- for his feedback, encouragement, and endless free advice provided during the writing of this book -- all served up with the utmost in consideration, patience, and 24/7 generosity. I only hope that I can someday repay your kindness, Mark. But I draw the line at organ donation.

I said kindness...not kidneys. Sara, I know the moustache is questionable...but keep him.

To Lawrence Knorr and everyone at Sunbury Press for all of their extraordinary efforts.

To all the grills I've loved before.

Table of Incontinence

Introduction

Food is an important part of most meals. We know where it's been...and we know where it's going. Wait a second, that didn't turn out exactly right.

Ahem.

Some people try to find the silver lining in everything. I try to find the food in everything. But it goes much deeper than that. In fact, it goes all the way down to the large intestine.

One of the most common intestinal disorders that affects people is called Diverticulitis -- more commonly known as an inflamed colon. This is not to be confused with MacGyverticulitis -- a similar condition which affects indiscriminate viewers of Prime Time network television. The exact cause of either affliction still isn't known for sure, but the symptoms are virtually identical. They include nausea, vomiting, fever, high temperature, cramping, constipation...and being utterly useless and annoying with a TV remote control.

After exhaustive internal research (research that analyzes a person's internal exhaust), most experts have determined that a diet high in fiber may be the answer. Remember this the next time you go to consult with a physician. Make sure you ask for a "High Fiber" specialist. Because if you mistakenly ask for a "High Fiver" specialist -- he'll end up shoving all five fingers up your ass. Afterwards he'll say "High Five!" and try to slap your hand in celebration. That's not what you want.

Everyone is familiar with The Last Supper. But what was in The First Supper? Don't bother flipping to the Table of Contents to find out the answer, either...because I honestly don't know what the contents were on their table. They might not even have used a table; they could have just eaten off of a big rock for all I know.

What I *can* tell you is that history's first popular superhero was not Superman. It was Supperman. Did he use Tupperware? No. Supperware.

Some say it all began with Adam and Eve and the Apple. To appear naked like that in public back then was certainly not very politically correct -- or, "PC". That's why they went and glued a bunch of fig leaves all over their bodies. Well, that, and because they were all out of Post-it Notes (Father, Son, and the Holy Ghost-it Notes?)

She was the apple of his eye...and with a little luck he would soon be deep in cider. Oh, how he pined for her fruity filling. He looked up to notice that they had been standing directly beneath that romantic, giant toe nail clipping in the sky (which many would consider a crescent moon). So he strung up a cot from one cedar to another cedar: it was a two-seater.

Of course, people of faith will tell you that God created Adam and Eve, not Adam and Steve. But then along came *Bill* and Steve with their own version of the Apple...and everything reverted back to being PC again. That is, until The Macintosh arrived.

What became of Adam? Sadly, Eve's constant bitching, nagging, and neglect finally succeeded in making him too indigested to "perform". That's right: he became a Bromosexual. Every night in bed, it was the same old torture for poor, unlucky Adam, as she would grumble: "Keep that snake to yourself, you pervert! What am I -- your own personal sex machine? Who do you think you are -- God's gift to women?"

You see, like many sexually repressed women of the time, Eve was partly cloudy...with chance of a biblical flood. I mean frigid.

Ironically, it was Adam himself who had provided Eve with her very first "aid" the previous Christmas in an effort to help her unwind. He had commissioned a wood carver to ensure that it perfectly resembled his own "Tree of Knowledge". Except that it was black. ("Yes, Vagina, there is a Santa Claus!")

Eve was so taken with the device that she would sometimes be up for 40 days and 40 nights hoping for the inevitable flood. Neighbors could hear her impassioned voice yelling: "Hallelujah! Hallelujah! Good God almighty! Come and take me, Lord! Oh, YES! I am ready to RECEIVE YOU!!!!" But they just assumed she was praying *really, really* hard.

Was it a marriage made in heaven? Actually...yes. But it wasn't long before Adam wanted to get the hell out of there. He had stopped taking Genesis seriously years ago. Even since before Peter Gabriel left.

Adam, who spoke mainly romance languages, languished on the shelf for quite a while. He would languish and languish and languish. One night, he got so lonely that he tried hitting on the Japanese woman who ran the local Fig Leaf Dry Cleaners up the street...in French. But she didn't speak the languish.

That rejection, combined with his fondness for eating with his shoes off, nearly caused him to become a Kimonosexual. Leaf Pressing has since evolved into a popular craft.

Ultimately, Adam's love of food drove him back into the kitchen...where he would eventually come out of the cupboards. I mean closet. (As it turns out, he had been concealing his love of cooking for years.)

Bill and Steve finally convinced Eve to change her Outlook. Which she did. For Hotmail. (*Lots* and *lots* of hot males would follow for Eve!)

And Adam had his humble kitchen to thank for it all. He had attended many baseball games over the years, where he witnessed stars such as Pete Rose, Nolan Ryan, Johnny Bench, Cal Ripken Jr., George Brett, and Steve Garvey get rushed on the field and openly flirted with by an outrageously sexy female admirer. It was Morganna the Kitchen Bandit.

Adam was so taken by her fondness for smooching that he immediately bought her a colorful, fresh bouquet and even wrote her a heartfelt poem:

Gladiola I could be here
With these Tulips for kissing.
If you're a spring flower,
Then I'm the biggest flower picker you ever planted one on.
And Roses led the children to the Promised Land.

As a gesture of his eternal gratitude to his cupboards, his new life's motto became, "To thine own shelf be true". That's why you should read this book. It appeals to not just one...but *two* sexes!

Now go stuff yourselves....

Generic Food Prayer

Our fodder, who art ingested,
halibut be thy name.
Thy king crab come,
thy will be gumbo,
unearthed, as it is in mushrooms.
Give us this day our breaded shrimp,
and forgive us our Triscuits and molasses,
as we foil-wrap those
who flapjack against us.
And lead us not into tempura,
but asparagus from evil.
For thine is the dim sum,
the flour, and the cacciatore.
For heifer and heifer.
Almond.

Reese's Pieces be with you (and also with you).

IT'S BEEN MORE THAN SIX HOURS HONEY, DON'T YOU THINK WE AUTA CALL A DOCTOR?
CAN'T WE KEEP IT?

Aphrodisiac Food

Men often wake up with an erection. I like to call it "Morning Thickness". It's just nature's way of telling the guy to take care of business before he leaves the house.

But it's not always that automatic. The situation doesn't always unfold itself to such a high peak. (For those poor men whose "situation" rarely unfolds itself, and are seldom able to maintain a high peak...consult with a qualified urologist immediately.)

Remember, reproduction is one of the prime Biological Imperatives. This is a code which all living organisms are bound by in order to successfully pass on their DNA. "Perpetuation of the Species" has been literally hard-wired (pardon the expression) into males over hundreds of millions of years. In that respect, we're no different from *The Terminator.* ("That's what he does. That's ALL he does!!!")

Similarly, females have been programmed by nature to be receptive and nurturing creatures. Well, there are exceptions. Like Tonya Harding. When Tonya used to go out nightclubbing -- she would actually bring a club.

And Courtney Love. Courtney once brought her ailing baby daughter in to a pediatrician for a long-overdue visit. The doctor determined she suffered from diaper rash, malnutrition, worms, jaundice, and colic. And the baby was in pretty rough shape, too.

So, you see, it's not unusual for men and women in the mood to have to reach out for a little assistance every now and again. After all, we live in a hurried and stressful age; distractions are good and plenty; and there are mounds of inhibitions that sometimes make you feel like a nut.

However, dialing 9-1-1 is *not* recommended. Not unless you want the cuffs slapped on you for lodging a nuisance call. Wait a second...*handcuffs*? Hmmmm! (Makes a mental note.)

An aphrodisiac is any food, drug, or substance that stimulates, arouses, or intensifies sexual desire. It is derived from "Aphrodite" -- the Greek goddess of love, beauty, and sexuality.

Sexuality in the brain is controlled by the Hypothalamus. This is an almond-sized structure located just above the brain stem (Almond Joy?). In fact, it is positioned almost directly in the center of your brain. How it got there remains one of life's greatest mysteries -- right up there with how they got the creamy caramel into the Caramello bar.

But for those who suffer from Edema (swelling of the brain), it's sometimes referred to as the "Hippopota-thalamus"; and these people are forced to try and cool their insatiable desire for hot sex by wading in ponds for up to ten hours a day. I mean the water body -- not the cold cream. Having said that...Pond's cold cream has been known to help alleviate the burning, itching, scaling, and other uncomfortable side effects typically associated with Pachydermatitis. Care should be taken that the water isn't too cold, however -- for that might result in a bad case of hippothermia.

People at various points in history were not nearly as well-nourished as most of us are today. Due to factors relating to poverty and class, many were under-fed, and suffered from various forms of malnutrition. People who happen to be well-fed are not only sounder of mind, body, and spirit, but they also boast a healthier libido...and greater potency. It's always been about potency.

The list of foods considered to possess aphrodisiac qualities is an ancient, varied, and international one. It includes: Almond, Aniseed, Apricots, Arugula, Asafetida, Asparagus, Avocado, Bananas, Basil, Carrots, Chocolate, Cloves, Coffee, Coriander, Fennel, Figs, Fugu (blowfish), Garlic, Ginger, Ginkgo Biloba, Ginseng, Honey, Liquorice, Mustard, Nutmeg, Oysters, Peaches, Pine Nuts, Pineapple,

Rapini, Raspberries, Sake, Strawberries, Truffles, Vanilla, and Wine.

That's right…blowfish. This deadly-poisonous critter has long been a Japanese delicacy. There's just one thing: if the expertly-trained chef makes a mistake and the blowfish isn't properly prepared…you'll drop dead on the spot of asphyxiation. (I wonder if that's their idea of a "to-go" order?) Maybe that's the real reason why a Japanese meal is traditionally eaten only after the shoes have been removed. This way, it's easier for the attending coroner to slip on a toe tag.

The ancient Aztecs called the avocado tree "Ahuacuatl," which translates to "testicle tree". In hindsight, "Hey you kids, get out of that Jell-O tree!" doesn't sound so bad.

Whether or not any of these foods actually does anything to boost your sex life is largely up for grabs. In which case, you'd be better off if you just went ahead and grabbed your ankles. To this day, most scientific studies have yet to find the presence of active ingredients of any kind. Sure, some foods may be high in protein, others in zinc, others in potassium and B vitamins, etc. -- all essential elements of a healthy diet, and, therefore, contributing factors to a good libido. But there is no "magic genie" in the lantern to speak of. It's more a matter of what's between the ears than the legs. Except for alcohol. Now, *that'll* get the hamsters running on the wheel!

Unfortunately, many Asian countries continue to import body parts that have been removed from highly endangered animal species in the misguided belief that they will help to improve their sex lives or increase potency. Rhinoceros horn, tiger penis, and shark fins are merely three examples. As a result, the wild populations of all three are being decimated at alarming rates.

There is nothing funny about this. (Author wags his finger sternly.) We should all shout out a collective "BOOOOO!" to the people who regularly dine on these disappearing natural wonders -- but mostly to their governments who stand idly by. Talk about *im*potent?

I fart in their general direction. And it sure doesn't smell like an aphrodisiac, I can assure you. (It smells more like a python doing the full Monty.)

By now, most people have been made aware of the fact that dolphins continue to be unfortunate by-catch victims of the tuna fishing industry. These playful, intelligent creatures have been known to come to the rescue of human beings who found themselves stranded in the ocean -- where the dolphins would protect them from sharks, drowning, and even escort them safely back to shore. They should never end up in a recipe. Especially one that recommends All-Porpoise flour.

But these nations also dine regularly on what hundreds of millions of Westerners would look at as their much-beloved and cherished family pets: namely, cats and dogs. Over there, if you say you're a "cat lover," or a "dog lover," it means something entirely different. And some of the meals look so life-like that they practically jump off the plate at you. That's why it's important to have a rabies shot before every meal. Or, at the very least, you should always dine with a rolled up newspaper beside you.

If you're ever strutting down an alley and happen to stray into a restaurant for a bite, be aware that cat dishes are a staple item. In fact, many are runaway favorites! But they don't sell them by the pound...they sell them *at* the pound. Popular cat dishes include:

- Furry Curry Chicken
- Cat on a Hot Tin Pie Plate
- Hiss and Chips
- Juicy and the Pussycats
- Kentucky Fried Kittens

Oh, and don't be embarrassed if you cough up a hairball after finishing eating. It's considered a compliment. But please stay off the furniture. ("Bad! Bad!")

Or, if dogs are more to your palate, you will find such disturbing menu items as:

- A Quarter-Hounder with Cheese

- Eggs (Pooched, and Rover-Easy)
- German Shepherd's Pie
- Uncle Benji's Converted Rice
- Mutt Mutton (served with Collie Greens)
- Chicken Noodle Snoopy
- Rack of Lab
- Yorkshire Terrier Pudding
- Dijon Frisé Mustard
- Spaniel-Flavor Cake Mix, from Betty Cocker
- Puppy Seed Bagels

Moreover, dinner is not referred to as "Din-Din"... but rather, "Rin-Tin-Tin". Instead of "Potluck"...they make "Spot" Luck. We cook with Fennel...they cook with Kennel. We serve Roughage...they serve "Ruff!"-age. We say "Dog Is Man's Best Friend"...they say, "Dinner *Was* Man's Best Friend". Men don't go to "Hooters"...they go to "Neuters".

Remember, some restaurants are better than others, so stick with the ones who have a rating of at least four paws out of five. And don't bother to retrieve the bill... they'll fetch it for you. These chefs give the term "Gallopping Gourmet" a whole new dimension.

The influence of Kitty-and-Canine cuisine is so tangible in these countries that it even helped pave the way for China's long-serving communist dictator, Chairman Meow, to ascend to power. Chairman Meow espoused "Meowism" -- which actually had nothing at all to do with politics. It was simply a guide for cooking and serving up cats. That same strong influence has even managed to heart-worm its way into their criminal justice system. Case in point: convicted criminals who are sentenced to death are not "executed"...they are "put down". But who are we to pass judgment on other cultures, anyway?

Animal experts have long maintained that the common pig is perhaps one of the smartest animals around, yet we eat them like they're going out of sty. I mean style. In fact, some of my favorite pork recipes are so secret, they're written down in invisible oink.

Furthermore, we eat cows...so why shouldn't other cultures be allowed to eat horses? (Especially if it's a losing horse who keeps costing you big at the race track. He deserves to die.) What's one man's Filet Mignon...is another man's Filly Mignon.

But perhaps the most popular, wide-spread, profitable, and enduring means of enhancing the libido has nothing at all to do with food. That's right...pornography. Porn is available in the form of books, movies, magazines, videos, DVD's, cable TV, and now the internet.

In 1991 in Florida, Pee Wee Herman was arrested for revealing his member in an adult movie theater. In Herman's defense -- he thought it was a Members Only club.

Oh, and what if somebody tells you to go screw yourself? Well, then in that case, what you'll need is a Hermaphrodisiac.

Food As Currency

The Ancient World

Soldiers in Ancient Rome were paid a "salarium argentum" which enabled them to receive a portion of salt.

"Salarium" means "salt".

"Argentum" means "white".

White money.

The word "salary" is derived from "salarium".

"Salarium" is different from "solarium" -- which means "sun room". To turn a room in your house into a solarium doesn't mean you'd fill it with salt -- for then you'd end up with a "Sodom & Gomorrium".

Ancient Greek slave traders would acquire slaves by paying for them with salt. A slave who didn't measure up was commonly denounced as being "not worth his salt". This works *way* better as an insult than calling someone "low sodium".

Around about 2,000 BC, Chinese Emperor Xia Yu was possibly the first known politician to institute a tax on his kingdom. But he didn't tax property or income. He taxed salt. He also went by the title "Yu the Great"...or just plain "Hey Yu!" to his friends.

Tea bricks were widely used as currency in Asia right up until the end of World War II. Of course, if you happened to be a coffee drinker, you'd be screwed, brewed, and tattooed. Building a house made of tea bricks was not recommended, however, because when it rained it would only be good for two cups, maximum. Then you'd have to wring the whole thing dry and go build another.

In fact, most early civilizations used food in place of money. The hardest part of any transaction was always having to remember to wash your hands first. And putting on that damn bib could be a real pain, too.

People would buy or trade for merchandise using whatever food items they happened to have on hand: wheat, rice, cattle, pigs, chickens, fruits, vegetables, or even wine. To barter effectively meant you had come as close as possible to the actual retail price without going over. For these types of serious negotiations, they would often call in a ringer known as a "Bob Barter". This man always seemed to know when the price was right -- right up until the day he died. (He fell over a steep cliff while yodeling.)

"I said the barter system, not the farter system!"

The problems inherent with offering up food as payment were numerous: food will spoil; crops often aren't available until the fall; animals die. As a result, metal money was invented: otherwise known as "coins". Coins could be mass-produced, they were portable, and they weren't dependent on the seasons or weather. They also made coin collections possible. From this point forward, food would forever be couched in coins. And who among us isn't thrilled to find coins in a couch?

North America

The oldest company in all of North America is "The Hudson's Bay Company". It was established in 1670, and is still headquartered in Toronto, Ontario, Canada.

"Toronto" is Mohawk for "where there are trees standing in the water." I obtained this morsel of knowledge from an obscure tribe called the "Couldashouldawoulda". Nice people -- they just keep putting things off.

"The Bay" controlled the fur trade throughout much of British-controlled North America for several centuries, making them instrumental in early exploration.

Since early settlements were sparse, there was very often no formal currency in circulation. As a result, the beaver pelt became adopted as the official unit of currency. Canadians have loved beaver ever since. Native Indians did much of the trapping and hunting, as well as acting as lookouts and guides. You could always trust a Native with your wife's beaver.

And if your wife had two or three beavers, he'd say you were the luckiest man in the world.

Beaver pelts were shipped back to England and France where they were used to make clothing and Top Hats. The process of making the felt for hats involved the use of the toxic chemical, mercury. Prolonged exposure to mercury would cause hat makers to go mad. (Or, perhaps it was prolonged exposure to people who wear Top Hats?) Hence, the expression, "Mad as a Hatter".

In addition to beaver pelts -- tobacco, wheat, peas, and corn were made legal tender across much of early North America. For the equivalent of a basket of fresh produce, a settler could even purchase the favors of a local prostitute. ("She may not have been legal...but she sure was tender!") Of course, if he wasn't careful, he might also catch any one of a number of STD's. (Be careful, guys...an "STD" is *not* a florist franchise.)

Unscrupulous sellers of corn who overcharged for their product were commonly denounced as "Buccaneers". Why? Because they charged a buck an ear.

Not only was deer meat used as barter, but their skins were also widely traded. Each deer skin was called a "buck". This eventually became the slang term we would adopt for "dollar".

It's a good thing they didn't trade desiccated buffalo penises. ("I've got twenty-five pricks burning a hole in my pocket!")

Here are some other foods which have been known to refer to money: Bread, cabbage, beans, bacon, beef, dough, lettuce, kale, bones, clams, coconuts, cheddar, peanuts, chicken feed, guacamole, mint, bananas, batter, beehives, biscuits, donuts, greens, hogs, corn, crust, cod's roe, macaroni, matzahs, mackerels, and crackers.

So if you weren't previously aware of the extent to which food and money have been traditionally linked like sausages, it's time to pour yourself a tall cup of reality... and wake up and smell the coffers!

Romantic Dinners

"Dinner and Drinks" are inextricably linked, save for one major caviar. I mean caveat.

Most marriage proposals occur over dinner.

Most divorce proposals occur over drinks.

Romantic Dinners can be divided into two main groups:

1. Those for single couples
2. Those for married couples

The difference between the two? It's a simple matter of "In-and-Out". Single couples look at dinner as a strategy of getting into bed...and into each other's arms. Married couples look at dinner as a strategy of getting out of the house ...and away from the kids.

In a Restaurant

The degree of interest that exists when ordering from the menu is directly proportional to the degree of interest that exists in the relationship.

Single couples often begin with an appetizer and like to savor each course with great relish.

Married couples lost their appetites years ago, and look down at their feet a lot as if they *stepped* in great relish.

Single couples will comment on every sizzling aspect of the restaurant experience -- including the food, the service, the clientele, and the ambiance.

Married couples will comment on how the single couples are making them sick to their stomach, and how they'd love to walk over there and punch them in the face.

At Home

Both men and women may take the initiative when planning a romantic dinner for two at home.

A woman might like to start the train rolling by leaving a sexy message on the man's answering machine. Or a sexy email on the man's email machine. She can deck out the table with an expensive table cloth and napkins, place dimly-lit candles around the room, and even sprinkle rose petals across the table.

A man might like to start the train rolling by actually having his model train rolling around his apartment. What says romance better than the occasional "Toot-Toot!" --accompanied by a corresponding puff of grey smoke? And what woman wouldn't be impressed with a man who goes to all the trouble of laying out a complete set of handsomely monogrammed napkins?

Of course, she might feel differently once she finds out that his initials aren't really "KFC".

Many men still resort to the ages-old strategy of conveniently "running out of gas" when driving their girlfriend home. This idea does not scream "genius," however, if you happen to be taking her home in a helicopter or plane.

Popping The Big Question

Marriage licenses first started being issued during the Middle Ages. For thousands of years before that, women were assigned to men as property. This was meant to improve the chances that the woman was not only a virgin, but that their children would be his and his alone. What does this tell us?

Well, it tells us a couple of things: 1. That men were incredibly insecure back then. 2. That women were hopping around from straw bed to straw bed like caffeinated jack rabbits.

Somebody had to lay down the law once and for all. Otherwise, men and women could conceivably have gone on and on into eternity constantly screwing around on each other. And that would be a bad thing, right?

This was most likely also the same time that the term "Extra Virgin Olive Oil" was first coined. For, what man wouldn't want his woman to be "Extra Virgin" who wasn't already insecure to begin with? "Extra Virgin": Does that mean she hasn't had sex *lots* of times?

Ah, isn't love wonderful? It's that eternal game of cat-and-mouse played being between the sexes.

But there arrives that crucial time in every relationship when the subject of eternal commitment must be addressed: it's time to pop the big question.

An engagement ring secretly placed at the bottom of a glass of white wine always works wonders. So does a wad of hundreds sticking out of your pocket.

Red wine is murkier, and therefore not as effective, because she may end up swallowing the ring. (If this happens, waiting for that ring to eventually turn up will be just like embarking on your own little adventurous treasure hunt! But if you plan on proposing while away on a camping trip for more than a few days, you might want to bring along a metal detector...and don't let her out of your sight.)

A man's stomach has long been referred to as "The Gateway to the West". Sorry, that's the Gateway Arch in St. Louis, Missouri.

"The way to a man's heart is through his stomach" is what I meant. And well worth remembering, I might add.

So, no matter what you're eating to mark this romantic night, just remember that love is a two-way street...not a tow-away zone. The two look dangerously similar, which is why it's important that you wear your glasses if you're nearsighted; because one will get you towed. And if I towed you once...I towed you a thousand times. (Being pounded by your sex-starved lover is a wonderful thing; being *impounded* is not.)

On Bended Knee

Men have been proposing from the bended knee position since the medieval era of English Knights. Bowing to a woman was a gesture indicating chivalry, respect, and compliance.

On the other hand, Robin Hood decided to dump Maid Marion because, as it turns out, she just wasn't made for marryin'.

There are other theories as to why men propose on bended knee, however. Some claim that it mirrors the exact position which a condemned prisoner is forced to assume right before he gets his head chopped off. Others take it as a man's sly way of letting the woman know that he'd like for her to be on top once in a while. Both equally romantic! For, what man wouldn't lose his head when presented with a little variety in the old sackaroony?

Food Spa

Although food is meant primarily for putting into your mouth (then chewing and swallowing), people have been using it for thousands of years in a vain -- and deveining -- attempt to beautify themselves.

We use eggs as shampoo

Eggs are said to make your hair softer, shinier, and more bouncy. They're also the perfect breakfast complement to people who use bacon in their hair. And what better way to save on waste when you have a leftover egg from an omelet than to pour it over your head? Just remember, the eggs should always be raw: hard-boiled or scrambled will just make you look ridiculous.

Nobody is really sure if eggs actually help your hair at all, but one thing is for sure: the toughest part is trying to fit your head into the frying pan.

We place cucumber or potato slices over our eyes as compresses to remove dark circles and reduce puffiness

Have you ever been at your favorite salad bar when somebody suddenly shoves their face into one of the giant bowls? You guessed it: dark circles and puffiness. It could happen to any one of us.

Many people also use tea bags for the same effect. Just as with eggs, nobody is really sure if tea bags actually help our eyes at all. But one thing is for sure: the toughest part is trying to fit your face into the pot.

We enjoy coffee enemas

A coffee enema is a healthful, therapeutic cleansing technique. The caffeine stimulates the liver to produce more bile; which emits toxins into the colon; which is then flushed from the system. ("Would you like regular blend or de-crappinated?") It's also a great way to get that extra kick out of caffeine that you so desperately crave in the morning. But thankfully, I don't think Coffee Enema Drive-Thru's will be catching on in a big way any time soon.

Cocoa butter has long been a preferred skin moisturizer by wrinkled prunes everywhere. What they don't realize is that if you add milk and sugar to cocoa butter...you end up with milk chocolate. That's why it's very important to never shower in milk and sugar after you've received a treatment; or you'll end up completely encased like that poor lady in *Goldfinger*. Except in this case, you'll look more like a Butterfinger.

Chocolate body wraps are becoming increasingly popular, as are chocolate pedicures. With pedicures, milk chocolate is always preferred over dark chocolate. If you see a lady with what appears to be dark chocolate, you can be pretty sure it's because her husband held her feet to the fire after finding out how much all this was costing.

Fruit extract facial peels are supposed to result in smoother, glowing skin. Apples seem to be the fruit of choice. However, if you do decide to opt for an apple concoction, make sure they have been properly de-bugged before you leave it sitting on your face for an hour. Nobody likes a woman with worm holes in her face.

Personal Grooming

Few people are aware of the fact that legendary mobster, Al Capone, was a huge fan of salons. In 1929 in Chicago, he treated seven of his most hated adversaries to "the works". You've heard of a "perm"? Well, what Al did to those guys was truly permanent. It became known as "The St. Valentine's Day Manicure". Lots of people got clipped. Say what you want about old Al, but he was a leader -- not a follicle.

Those unsuspecting victims left the house that day thinking they were going to receive a complimentary round of golf. In fact, what Capone told his henchman was: "give those rotten bastards 18 holes apiece."

Capone was merely one in a long line of appearance-conscious mobsters throughout the 20th century who believed in looking the part. They wouldn't be fully good to go until they'd applied generous portions of Dep gel to their hair in order to achieve that all-important, picture-perfect, razor-thin part (Til Dep do us part?). Not surprisingly, as a result of their devotion to six course meals, cold cuts, cannoli, and lack of exercise...many of these tubbies would end up in the Fitness Protection Program. Many more were simply accessories after the fat.

Capone himself had a voracious appetite. He could suck the seeds right out of an apple...without even biting the apple. In high school he was voted "most likely to suck seeds".

While mowing my lawn one day, I stopped for a friendly chat with the mailman who delivers on my street. He threw me for a loop when he mentioned how he believed that my house might be haunted. When I asked him what could possibly ever lead him to believe that my house was haunted, he replied that he had innocently peeked in through the living room window one day, only to witness an eerie female apparition slowly shuffling along the floor with both arms outstretched in front of her: not unlike a sleepwalking ghost.

"Was that a gorgon I saw? A sea hag? A vampire?" he asked.

"No," I mumbled. "That was just my wife drying her nails."

Back when I was 19 and still waiting for my skin to clear up, I had been in a nightclub partying modestly with some friends, when an incredibly attractive girl approached me. She bounced over with a warm, receptive smile, and immediately began to make small talk. It was clear to everyone around us that she was practically all over me -- much to my shock, amazement, and surprise.

Then she said: "I just love your goatee. It's so sexy, full, and shiny. How do you get it to look like that?"

That wasn't a goatee. Those were blackheads.

Portable Food

Canned foods helped to facilitate the spread of civilization across the United States and Canada. At the behest of Napoleon himself, the technique of preserving foods was invented in France around 1809. This was done in an effort to improve the war effort by delivering food to its soldiers in a more expedient fashion. The process used air-tight glass jars which were then heated to kill any bacteria. In 1811, England enhanced the process by introducing tinned iron, which was certainly more resilient than glass.

By 1815, the technology spread to the rest of Europe and North America following the end of the Napoleonic Wars. Glass would still be preferred over tin for making glass eyes, though.

The next time you see a picture of Napoleon with his hand inside his coat? He's hiding a cold beer. "War effort," my ass! He loved being able to sip on a cold one while walking around the Eiffel Tower (being that the tower is such an eyeful).

The large-scale introduction of canned foods allowed early North American settlers to embark on long expeditions like never before. And thus, two great countries were forged. In fact, some believe that's why it's called "Canada" in the first place: those wacky Canadians just loved everything about canned foods. But mostly, they made good emergency hockey pucks when there were no cows around to drop a few.

You've heard of a referee "dropping the puck"? Well the original refs were cows. Otherwise, the country could just as easily have been named "Glassada," "Potteryda," or, just plain "Duh".

The EYEFUL Tower

In the United States, the use of tin cans would help pave the way for an explosion of popular culture. Can you imagine Popeye trying to open up a *glass jar* of spinach? And then, the lid won't turn, so he has to tap around the rim with a knife handle to loosen it up? It just doesn't pack the same wallop that a concentrated stream of powerful green spinach bursting out of a can directly into his mouth does...now does it? Plus, you'll notice that the can always bends from the pressure exerted by his mighty hand. If that was glass, it would simply have shattered to pieces in Popeye's hand. Not only would Popeye have required constant medical attention for his badly gashed hand...he likely would have starved to death, too. Happy now?

And similarly, what if Andy Warhol had been relegated to painting milk bottles instead of soup cans? Oh, how history would have been so much poorer for it.

Sure, there's always plastic -- but there's hardly anything romantic about plastic, either. You've never heard of somebody keeping their valuable coin collection in a grocery store bag, have you? No, of course not: it was empty cigar tins, cookie canisters, or coffee containers all the way; or, kids storing their treasured bubble gum cards inside a clear zip-lock sandwich bag? Heresy. Besides... "One Tin Soldier" is a helluva lot easier to sing than "One Plastic Soldier".

Not only that, but many of our favorite rock bands were "Heavy Metal". I challenge you to name me any that were "Heavy Plastic". OK...Emerson, Lake, and Polymer. I'll give you that one.

Food For Babies

Think of a placenta as Baby's first room. Babies in the uterus receive nourishment through their mother's umbilical cord by way of the placenta. The placenta is a sack which provides the baby with blood, oxygen, nutrients... and rudimentary baby toys to help shut them up so we can get some sleep. The baby's waste products are excreted back into the placenta where they are promptly carried away by the mother's blood.

Thus, "Clean your room!" and, "Why can't you pick up after yourself, you ungrateful, lazy slob!" are expressions that are ingrained in us from an early age: from before we can speak, even. As it turns out, Mom was cleaning up after us *since before we were even born*! Wow -- talk about your lost causes? This is truly an argument we can never win against dear old Mom. It is at precisely this stage where the whole blessed concept of "Mom" begins.

It also marks what is quite possibly the most celebrated example of a mother and child reunion in human history. At least up until 1972, anyway -- that's when Paul Simon topped the charts with his famous song of the same name. Simon had only recently served his fuzzy-headed-ingrate-of-a partner his walking papers: i.e. Garfunkel got "Simonized". Justifiably so, since Simon wrote all the songs and was the creative force behind all the hot wax.

To this very day, most people think that "Bridge Over Troubled Water" is a song about love and devotion. Wrong. It's an homage to the umbilical cord. The original lyric was "Bridge Over Amniotic Fluid". That was soon changed to "Bridge When Your Troubled Water Breaks". But once the song was eventually recorded, it wasn't released due to contractual obligations, exactly -- but, rather, *contraction* obligations. In other words, it just *had* to come out, no matter what. Record company executives were practically lined up yelling "Push! Push!" to get it into the record stores. This prolific and reproductive period in pop music history -- perhaps the most fertile ever -- was bursting over with poignant nods to pregnancy. These compositions were labors of love; even if the labor was sometimes induced.

In 1967, Glen Campbell scored big with the gentle ballad: "By The Time I Get To Fetus".

The Doobie Brothers went gold in 1973 with their energetic rocker, "Vagina Grove".

In 1974, Bo Donaldson and the Heywoods widened their stance considerably with "Belly Don't Be A Hero".

In 1975, Elton John paid tribute to the important role that nurses play in the birthing process, with the hair-razing, "Someone Shaved My Wife Tonight". (Speaking of women who show up at the hospital with a bush that is inordinately overgrown, dense, and entangled -- Elton also sang about how it sometimes takes nurses a jungle machete to hack their way through them: "Safari Seems to be the Hardest Word". Either way...these brave nurses risk significant personal injury every time they attempt such an invasive and ticklish ritual: because hell hath no fury like a woman shorn.)

Kansas came out swinging in 1976 with "Caesarean My Wayward Son". It was a painless cut that came not one second premature.

Still others would celebrate the precious miracle of conception.

In 1967, Herman and the Hermits boasted a largely prepubescent and impressionable young fan base, which made the band very reluctant to use the word "Beaver" in a song. So, instead, they released "Mrs. Brown You've Got A Lovely Otter".

In that same year, Frankie Valli had a summertime smash with "Can't Take My Thighs Off You".

The quintessential era of accidental pregnancies would be further memorialized in 1970, with the bluestinged moans of B.B. King's, "The Pill Is Gone". But don't turn that dial!

In 1971, the Bee Gees posed the timeless question: "How Can You Mend A Broken Condom?"

Roberta Flack hit #1 in 1973 with her haunting lament, "Killing Me Softly With His Schlong".

One year later, Steely Dan remained hard and strong, and proved they had lasting power with "Rikkie Don't Lose That Lumber".

The Police broke virgin ground in 1979 with their reggae-influenced, "Sausage In A Bottle," and "Walking On The Poon". Isn't music wonderful? And so sentimental!

Aviation buffs and mothers agree that flying an airplane and having a baby are two of the greatest natural highs a person could ever hope to experience. Having said that, a "Baby Boom" should never be confused with a "Sonic Boom". They mean something completely different. A Baby Boom is NOT the exploding sound a newborn baby makes as it rockets through the labia at the speed of sound.

Oh, well, what can you do? People are going to get knocked up -- just like my grandmother always said. But it's been a fun nine months, kid, and now it's time to stop leeching off your mother and get born, already.

So, what are these slobbering little gnomes going to do for food now that they're alive and breathing on their own? Enter tits. Cow tits. Bubble gum bubble tits. Round tits. Pointy tits. Ski-slope tits. Tits that sit high. Tits that hang low. Taffy pull nipples. Pimple nipples. 45-rpm areolas. Happy tits. Sad tits. Perky tits. Droopy tits. Fresh tits. Stale tits. Sexy tits. Shy tits. Functional tits. Professional tits. Amateur tits. Bouncy tits. *Really* bouncy tits. Established tits. Debutante tits. Veiny tits. Stretch mark tits. I'm-wearing-this-skimpy-top-because-I-really-want-to-land-that-high-paying-job tits. Porcelain tits. Black tits. Tan line tits. Peek-a-boo tits. Braless tits. He-went-that-a-way tits. Nice-tits-shame-about-her-face tits. Honk-Honk tits. Beep-Beep tits. Holy-Moly tits. I'll-tell-you-that-you-have-nice-tits-anyway-because-I-know-that's-what-you-want-to-hear-even-though-they're-really-not tits. Fillsup-your-blouse tits. Is-there-anybody-in-there tits. Right Wing nut cluster tits (over-the-shoulder-Coulter-holder). Liberal tits (Areola Huffington).

(Speaking of Ann Coulter...I think she should change her name to “Amanda”. Why? Because she looks like a man, duh!)

Some will tell you that it’s all downhill from there: a booby trap; a slippery slope down the mother of slippery slopes.

Babies generally stop breastfeeding at around 6 months old, or until their first tooth arrives. Male babies, however, will go on to fantasize about possibly reacquiring the practice again at around age 14, or until their first erection arrives. And while mothers often experience “Postpartum” depression after childbirth, male babies who are suddenly robbed of tasty knockers to feast on are commonly subject to “Post Dolly Parton” depression.

In 1928 the Gerber baby food company held a national contest to find the cutest baby for an upcoming marketing campaign. A charcoal sketching of five-month old Ann Turner was chosen the winner, and the “Gerber Baby” was born. The Gerber Baby soon became part of Americana. What many people don’t know is that she came dangerously close to being known as the “Burger Baby”...because it seems lot of people suffered from dyslexia back then.

“Burger Baby” sounds way more in tune with the current generation of young people, especially considering the amount of morbidly obese fat kids we observe crushing our poor, unfortunate school buses with their gargantuan guts and barn door butts -- on their way to a tour of the Hershey’s plant while they eat donuts from a box and sing campfire songs (“Force, force, force your cake, gently down your throat -- Sara Lee, Sara Lee, Sara Lee, Sara Lee, life is but a bloat.”) These perpetually half-winded water buffalos can “like-really” relate to *The Sopranos*, because, like Tony, Paulie, Silvio, Christopher, Phil Leotardo, and Johnny Sack...they’re always asking for a “sit-down”. They generally refrain from ever giving each other the finger, however, because the longer it stays up, the more it begins to resemble a bread stick....and then they invariably try to eat it.

Baby formula is an indispensable addition to any baby's diet, although the very name itself -- "Formula" -- always conjures up disturbing notions of Dr. Jekyll and Mr. Hyde -- complete with wild eyes and a Top Hat, shuffling around all hunched over with a crooked limp, while scaling rooftops in dingy old London. Not exactly the mental image you want of your little angel as you tuck him or her in for the night. No. They shouldn't call it Formula -- anymore than they should use a Boris Karloff impersonator in their TV ads. ("Igor... bring me the Formula!")

Mashed fruits and vegetables (such as carrots, peas, pears, applesauce, and bananas) are easy, cheap, and versatile -- just like the baby's whore-face mother. She's the one who got you into this whole stinking mess in the first place.

Finally, it goes without saying that great care should be taken when selecting a qualified and capable physician for your baby. Try to avoid anyone who attained their medical degree online. Or, in other words: a Wikipediatrician.

Food In Literature

(From Dickens to Dickinson,
From Stein to Steinbeck to Frankenstein)

Contrary to popular belief, Plato did not invent the plate. (Or Play-Doh.) Socrates was the teacher of Plato. Plato was mentor to Aristotle. Together, they helped found modern philosophy, science, and logic. They were "The Three Greeks". Sort of like "The Three Tenors"...but a hell of a lot slimmer. Their names are so intertwined, that if you combine the name "Aristotle" with "Socrates"...you end up with "Artistocracies". The fact that three Greeks could agree on anything must be some kind of a record. But like plates in Greece...records are meant to be broken. So, no, Plato did not invent the plate.

And neither did Chaucer invent the saucer. Chaucer's *Canterbury Tales* (late 14th Century) includes a story called "The Knight's Tale". This classic tale of friendship turned bitter as the result of rival affection for a fair maiden was written in iambic pentameter. Upon hearing this, Sarah Palin remarked: "Ah, it was written in Iambic, Pentameter, huh? That must be in Asia somewhere, right? I don't think I've ever visited there. Which part of the world is 'Iambic, Pentameter'? Can somebody find that out for me in case it comes up in my next interview with Katie Couric?"

Some might say that Sarah Palin is just plum stupid. In fact, Sarah Palin and Joe the Plumber should run together as Republicans: they can call themselves "Plum and Plumber". (Their theme song could be, "He'll be plumbing round the mountain when she comes.")

Horace and Virgil were the two predominant poets in Ancient Rome. It was Horace who coined the phrase "carpe diem" ("seize the day"). Unfortunately, somebody misheard him, and thought he said "carpet diem" ("seize the rug"). Well, nobody likes a carpet thief.

When Caesar (who wore a rug) found this out, he immediately tried to have Horace whacked -- believing that Horace had finally gone too far and worn out his welcome mat.

Virgil implored Horace to escape down to the river and get the heck out of town. But Horace was steadfast and refused to budge. Which only goes to show: you can lead a Horace to water....

What types of food were eaten in Shakespeare's time? The list included: mutton, lamb, cheese, beans, wild boar, berries, fruits, grapes, beer, wine, and various game birds (like pheasants) which were of the partridge family. (Long Live The Partridge Family!) The menu items were *As You Like It*; because if you *didn't* like it, the restaurant staff would order you drawn and quartered. And by that, I don't mean they would have an artist sketch you and then pelt you with quarters

Shakespeare grew up in "Tudor England". This was when cars were in their infancy -- long before the era of "Four Door England," or "Station Wagon England". A budding guitar player, Shakespeare lived in Stratford... because he loved to play his Strat.

Shakespeare performed many of his most famous plays at the Globe Theater. "The Globe" was a theater-in-the-round which held between 2,000 and 3,000 spectators. Probably the most important aspect of the theater was that it was "Open-Air". This was no mere accident. Mainly because most of the patrons lived on a steady diet of beer, beans, and cheese. But due to their heavy drinking and rowdy behavior, many wound up "bard" for life.

Edward Gibbon's *The History of the Decline and Fall of the Roman Empire* (1776) remains one of the highest-selling books ever. At the time, Britain was a rather unsanitary place in which to live. Residents would throw their raw, untreated sewage out into the streets or directly into the Thames River. Much of the available food was infested with bacteria.

Bacteria would cause dysentery, which in turn would result in diarrhea. Most people in those days were of very modest means and didn't have a lot of money to spend unnecessarily. Therefore, when presented with the choice, they found it difficult to decide whether to buy a loved one a meal infested with bacteria, or a copy of *The History of the Decline and Fall of the Roman Empire.* Of course, most felt that a book was a hell of a lot more desirable than a bad case of diarrhea.

So, whichever way you ended up choosing -- whether the food or the book: it was the gift that kept on Gibbon.

Charles Dickens was the most popular novelist in the Victoria era. *Oliver Twist* (1838) is the story of a boy of the same name who lived and toiled in a workhouse for the poverty-stricken. One day Oliver lost a bet and was forced to ask the evil headmaster for more gruel (for it was a very grueling existence), "Please, sir, I want some more".

In *A Christmas Carol* (1843), the crotchety Ebenezer Scrooge is visited by the long-deceased Jacob Marley in what appears to be a grotesque hallucination. This would not be the last time that the name "Marley" would be associated with something resembling a marijuana-induced haze (The Ghost of Christmas Rasta?). In fact, just the mere mention of the name "Marley" was enough to fill Scrooge with dreadlocks. But the story became wildly popular, ensuring that Scrooge and Marley would keep readers in suspense -- and munchies! -- for years to come.

Ebeneezer Scrooge insisted that his fiancé, Belle, never wear a bra during the holidays. Every morning when she dressed, she'd shoot a quick glance over at him for his approval, and he would inevitably say, "Bra! Humbug!" The term evolved...and a cherished tradition was born. But walking around topless like that was always risky, since there were usually so many peeping Toms lurking about.

"The GHOST OF CHRISTMAS RASTA".

Belle liked to earn extra money by working as a tutor. But the children had such a hard time concentrating on their lessons, what with her "one-horse, open sleighs" bouncing around the way they did. So Ebeneezer finally relented, and allowed her to throw on a T-shirt until the class was dismissed. Thrilled at the prospect of finally being able to concentrate on their studies, the children celebrated their victory by dousing her with Gatorade.

Everybody got what they wanted... and the "Wet Teacher Contest" was born.

Edgar Allan Poe was an editor, a critic, and a master of the macabre and science-fiction. He is also credited with inventing detective-fiction. But he started out by writing lots and lots of Edgar Allan Poetry. His most famous Edgar Allan Poem was "The Raven" (1845).

Poe was a tortured soul who died destitute and penniless. His health was always lacking due to chronic alcoholism and terrible eating habits. As a result, he suffered from a spastic colon and IVS (Irritable Vowel Syndrome). This caused him to spend endless hours sequestered in the bathroom of his dilapidated house, where he could be heard repeatedly flushing the toilet.

After years of this kind of abuse, the very foundation of the house finally gave way from the strain... causing it to collapse to the ground. This became the inspiration for one of Poe's greatest short stories, "The Fall of the House of Flusher" (1839).

Emily Dickinson was a poet and a hermit. She revolutionized poetry by employing unusual punctuations, and she rarely titled her poems. But mostly, she was famous for popularizing "slant rhymes"; that is, rhymes that don't *really* rhyme.

For example, here is an excerpt of a poem she wrote about mushrooms:

Had nature any outcast face,
Could she a son contemn,
Had nature an Iscariot,
That mushroom, -- it is him.

Here's another about an apple tree:

A DROP fell on the apple tree
Another on the roof,
A half a dozen kissed the eaves,
And made the gables laugh.

And here's yet another about a wounded deer:

A WOUNDED deer leaps highest,
I've heard the hunter tell;
'Tis but the ecstasy of death,
And then the brake is still.

The moral? Well, I'm no expert on poetry or anything, but the moral seems pretty obvious to me: wild venison meat is best served with a mushroom and apple sauce.

Henry David Thoreau was a poet, a tax resister, an anarchist, a naturalist... and a Thoreau pain in the ass. When he refused to pay his taxes on moral grounds, he was promptly thrown in jail -- leaving him *Thoreauly* embarrassed. He was bailed out against his wishes, for he was intent on using his imprisonment as a political statement. He left jail after serving only one day.

As he was leaving, the jail guards announced, "Parting is such sweet Thoreau". Thoreau wrote the landmark essay, "Civil Disobedience" (1849), which espouses non violent resistance (as opposed to resisting violent spouses). This work was to have great influence on Martin Luther King Jr., John Kennedy, and Mahatma Ghandi, among many others. Thoreau was friends with fellow Massachusetts residents (and lovers of New England Clam Chowder) Ralph Waldo Emerson, and Nathaniel Hawthorne.

Emerson was a poet, essayist, philosopher, transcendentalist, and individualist. He was also a big hit in crowds -- but notoriously difficult to find when you needed him. People would roam around all day asking, "where's Waldo?" Hawthorn wrote the novel, *The Scarlet Letter* (1850). The story is about a lady who commits adultery and is forced to wear a big red "A" on her chest.

Ostracized from the community, she would wander around for years and years, desperately looking to connect with a soul-mate, and someone who shared her peculiar fashion sense. She would find him in 1938. Yes, that's right...Superman. (Note: "Ostracized" means that a person has been excluded from a group. It does *not* mean that an ostrich has been circumcised.)

In 1881 Mark Twain released a novel about two young boys with an amazing resemblance who decided to play a prank by exchanging their identities. One was a prince who had zits; the other was a peasant who would pop them. Hence, *The Prince and the Popper* was born. Not coincidentally, the Popper lived in Offal Court, where he would regularly dine on, you guessed it...haggis (being that there was offal everywhere, which made it a rather offal place to live).

In 1883, Robert Louis Stevenson released *Treasure Island* -- a swashbuckling tale of pirates and buried treasure. This book introduced many icons which would forevermore come to be associated with pirates -- including peg-legged sailors with parrots on their shoulders, buried treasure, and a map marked with an "x" (just like the ones found at your favorite family restaurant). Although the book was fiction, it did mention several real-life pirates from history, including the notorious Blackbeard (real name: Edward Teach).

Many people are curious as to how Blackbeard acquired his nickname. Truth is, he was totally clean-shaven at the time he was given the ominous handle. You see, Blackbeard had spent some time pillaging in Europe -- and European women are famous for not shaving their body hair. So whenever he would go down on one of them...he looked like he had a black beard.

Rudyard Kipling wrote *Gunga Din* (1892), and *The Jungle Book* (1894). Kipling became famous as a pioneer of the short story. In kipling with his love of children's literature and wildlife, *The Jungle Book* came with a full monkey-back guarantee.

Bram Stoker gave the world the immortal "Count Dracula" in 1897. The title character underwent several revisions before Stoker finally settled on the definitive treatment.

Originally, he was "Vlad the Inhaler" -- a 15th Century Romanian prince with a serious marijuana and cocaine dependency.

Next, he was "Count Jocular" -- a jovial, wise-cracking, and happy-go-lucky creature of the night. Count

Jocular would wear down his unsuspecting victims -- not by hypnosis or brute force -- but by getting them to laugh so hard at his jokes to the point where they were rendered too exhausted to resist his advances. He would then zero in while his victims were still holding their stomachs and yelling, “Stop with the jokes, already! You’re killing me over here!” But Stoker realized that a vampire who would giggle and chuckle while slurping blood out of somebody’s throat would probably not be considered very scary.

After that, he appeared as “Count Spatula” -- a vampire who was also a gourmet cook. But a really *accomplished* gourmet cook...not just some Johnny-come-ladle. Stoker got the idea after seeing another vicious, relentless, terrorizing, and profane bloodsucker -- an English devil named Gordon Ramsay. Ramsay even had a show called “Ramsay’s Kitchen Nightmares”. How perfect was that?

And now on to O. Henry, writer of *Gift of the Magi* (1906). Remember how Gene Wilder insisted that his name is pronounced, not “Frankenstein,” but, rather, “Fronkensteen”? Well the “O” in “O. Henry” is actually not an “O”...it’s a zero. It should be pronounced “Zero Henry”.

Truth be told, “O. Henry” is merely a pen name. His real name is William Sydney Porter. But that would have looked ridiculous on a chocolate bar.

The practice of replacing your middle name with your favorite food was something that would never really catch on in the literary world. Most observers felt it made you sound ridiculous...and quite full of yourself. The tradition pretty much began and ended with Edgar Rice Burroughs, writer of *Tarzan* (1914). Burroughs had ruled out “Sheep’s Liver,” and “Cabbage,” before ultimately settling on “Rice”.

Similarly, the practice of replacing your middle name with your religion was even *more* frowned upon, as it tended to divide people. That tradition pretty much began and ended with Hans Christian Anderson. Later generations would give it a go, however, with short-lived attempts by Gertrude Jew-Face-Christ-Killer Stein, Mario Roman-Catholic-And-Thereby-An-Enabler-Of-Pedophile-Priests Puzo, and Christopher Atheist-Heretic-Who-Will-Burn-In-Hell Hitchens.

Before (and even during) her tenure as Prime Minister of Israel, Golda Meir was also a known and respected author. A tough-as-nails, no-nonsense negotiator, she quickly became known in political circles as, "My ass! My foot! My eye!" Meir.

L. Frank Baum wrote the legendary *The Wonderful Wizard of Oz* in 1900. He stuck an "L" at the beginning of his name. Otherwise, he would have been known as the "F" Baum.

Somerset Maugham was infatuated with Jonathan Swift's wife Lilly, and had been aggressively pursuing her -- against the fine lady's wishes. Somerset had always considered himself to be somewhat of a man about the kitchen. In fact, he just couldn't leave Lilly put. As a result, Jonathan gave Maugham a Swift kick in the *gulliver*. He had kicked his dad before...but never Maugham.

Maughan is also famous for having written *Of Human Bondage* (1915). Years later, Ian Fleming considered adapting the title when he wrote a story about a heroic and dashing British agent (nicknamed "007") who happened to possess kinky sexual fetishes involving S & M. It was to be called *Of James Bondage.*

James had a license to thrill. And after receiving a penile implant, he then became known as "008½".

Many popular American writers from the 1800s on up were born and raised on humble family farms. Take John Steinbeck, for example. Every morning, Steinbeck was up at the crack of Dawn. Dawn was his wife (who liked to sleep sideways).

Their days would be spent out in the pasture -- unless it was pasture bedtime, in which case they'd wait for the cows to come home. If you owned a farm, it was a very noble thing to have a barn. This is not to say that all barn owners were nobles. In fact, the opposite was true -- they were just average, regular people.

Luckily, barns and nobles learned to get along. They would combine their forces to showcase some of the most delectable writers of our time. On one particular occasion, they decided to erect a handsome display and stock it with books by Charles M. Schultz and J.K. Rowling on the outer panels, and Mary Shelley in the middle. The result was a Peanut, Potter, and Shelley sandwich.

J.K. has been Rowling in the dough ever since.

A.A. Milne was one honey of a writer. Talent oozed from his pores as though he was a giant buttered English Muffin. But alas, he was a lazy bugger. Still, everybody knew that he had what it took to become a success...if he could ever get his Pooh together.

The beloved character “Rabbit” was a smart, well-organized bunny that all the other animals admired. That being said, he was often hard to locate. That’s because he would spend literally days at a time stuffed down his girlfriend’s hole.

Milne’s unique name would become an inspiration for many -- including B.B. King, C.C. Rider, Dee Dee Ramone, J.J. Cale, LL Cool J, S.S. Minnow, ZZ Top, and other people of letters. Milne was generally thought of as a neigh-sayer. But if you would only get off his back, he’d usually emit a friendly whinny.

George Orwell was...well, Orwellian. His keen awareness of social injustice caused him to give serious consideration to the price of his books -- which he wanted to always remain affordable, and never overpriced. He decided they should cost no more than $19.84. Meanwhile, back on the animal farm, all the hungry employees had been eying a particularly juicy young pig. It had been days since anybody had eaten. That poor pig didn’t stand a Snowball’s chance.

British novelist, Sax Rohmer (real name: Arthur Henry Sarsfield Ward), first introduced his literary character, "Dr. Fu Manchu" in 1913. The character's name was actually "Tofu" Manchu. Tofu was a big hit on the competitive eating contest circuit. Fans would egg-roll him on by yelling "Chew, man, chew!". This would eventually get shortened to "Manchu".

The book *National Velvet* was released by author, Enid Bagnold, in 1935. Then, in 1944, the movie version was produced, which starred Elizabeth Taylor. Taylor (who was no stranger to calories) recounted the experience some years later. "Most people don't realize that the name of the horse in *National Velvet* was 'The Pie'. Well, I assumed that the director was trying to tell me something...so I ate him. He was delicious!"

Sadly, this would not be the last time that Ms. Taylor would eat a horse. For, career-wise, especially -- she was off to the races. Elizabeth Taylor puts the "gorge" back in gorgeous (and the "moo" back in movies). In addition to winning two "Best Actress" Oscars...she also won the Oscar for "Best Actress in Support Hose" an incredible 16 times!

In 1954, J.R.R. Tolkien released *Lord of the Rings.* The main character, Frodo, was known for Tolkien out of both sides of his mouth; a terrible habit, since it would cause whatever food he was eating to fall out all over his shirt. When Leo Tolstoy (author of *War and Peace*) arrived in America to visit Tolkien, he unexpectedly encountered a toll booth, where he discovered he had no tokens. So Tolstoy called up Tolkien who quickly brought him a token and the two went off toking.

Tolstoy also wrote *Anna Karenina* (1873). Out of admiration for his favorite bandleader, Lawrence Welk, Leo originally intended to make two versions: Anna1, Anna2

Norman Mailer was the total package. But he never mailed it in. He absolutely loved women. Whenever he went to a woman's apartment, it meant that his package would absolute, positively have to be there overnight.

He had testosterone enough to fill a cornucopia. This may explain the large bulge in his "Executioner's Thong". As time went on, and he got older, his masculinity would never wane. He just became *maler* and *maler.*

Sylvia Plath and John Steinbeck were rumored to have had a tumultuous secret love affair. Steinbeck, author of *The Grapes of Wrath* (1939), considered naming the book *The Grapes of Plath,* after Sylvia. When he didn't, Plath ended up committing suicide. It was a clear case of sour *Grapes* all the way.

In trying to pick up the stems and move on, Steinbeck concluded that Sylvia was way too much of a head case for his liking. In the future, he wanted a woman who was a little less...*world-weary.* Afterward, Steinbeck would take up with Sylvia's less-complicated sister. She was fondly regarded by her family members as being the Plath less traveled.

In 1962, Anthony Burgess unleashed *Clockwork Orange* upon the world. It was a futuristic tale about violence versus free will. The controversial movie version would follow in 1971. The name of the lead character was "Alex de Large". Hence, the Large orange juice was born.

In fact there was a sign in Burgess's office which read: "WARNING: Trespassers Will Be Reconstituted!" In the book, Alex and his thuggish mates refer to themselves as "Droogs". Very fitting -- because in order to understand this wacky book, it helps if you're very high on droogs.

Slaughterhouse 5 (1969) is an anti-war science fiction novel by Kurt Vonnegut. Vonnegut was intent on counteracting the prevailing public opinion that a slaughterhouse was somehow a hilarious and laugh-riotous place to be. He blamed this perception on the legendary comedy team of Abattoir and Costello. Throughout the 1940's and 50's, Abattoir and Costello were America's most popular comedy duo.

A triple-threat on radio, television, and films, their endearing routines were like fresh meat to the starving masses. Even though they were constantly on the hook to deliver, they would never fail to come up with Grade A material. Get a life, Kurt.

In 1974, author Peter Benchley would provide the world with the ultimate nickname for over-eaters: *Jaws*.

"Just when you thought it was safe to go back in the fridge..."

Author Douglas Adams released *Hitchhiker's Guide to the Galaxy* in 1979. It was a science-fiction tale involving aliens and outer space. This is not to be confused with *Hitchhiker's Guide to the Ford Galaxy* -- which is a tedious, true-life account of a boring soccer mom driving home her three wretched kids in a mini-van stuffed with the family groceries.

Historical Figures And Food

Burrito Mussolini
(1883-1945)
(Italian Fascist Dictator)

Between the years 1938-1945, Burrito ruled Italy with an iron ham-fist. As World War II was nearing last call, and he could see that the writing was on the chalkboard menu, Burrito tried to bounce out of Italy like a Mexican jumping bean. He was nabbed trying to cross the border into Switzerland. Both he and his mistress were shot and then strung up in a public square in Milan like a couple of Neapolitan piñatas.

Very ironic -- since the piñata was invented by another famous Italian way back in the 13th Century: the legendary sailor and explorer, Marco Polo.

Fiddle Faddle Castro
(1926 --)
(Cuban Dictator)

By December, 1958, Fiddle Faddle and his band of crackerjack revolutionaries had succeeded in overthrowing the corrupt Batista government. While initially assuring the world that Cuba would become a democracy, he quickly developed sticky fingers and became a communist dictator instead. Always one to come through in the crunch, Fiddle Faddle was not one to candy coat anything, and preferred to think outside of the box. But not everyone was fooled by his syrupy exterior. Many critics always felt he might be nuts underneath.

Ho Chi Mint
(1890-1969)
(Vietnamese Revolutionary)

The former capital of South Vietnam, "Saigon," was renamed "Ho Chi Mint City" on May 1, 1975, once the war ended. Although not a beefy man by any means, Mint refused to go along with imperialist pigs, obnoxious cows, or anyone who was chicken-hearted. But he did go great with lamb! The Ho Chi Mint trail was built in 1959 to speed up the war...but it was also said to leave a delightful minty smell. Mint was not your garden-variety wallflower. He had deep roots, and knew how to weed out traitors and pansies.

Vladimir Poutine
(1952 --)
(Russian Prime Minister)

This popular Russian politician was formerly President of the Russian Federation for two terms. Since nobody is permitted to rule for longer than that, he was promptly nominated for his current position as Prime Minister. Kurdish people throughout Europe began flocking to Russia in the year 2000 when they heard the new President loves Kurds. In reality, Poutine loves *curds* -- which he sprinkles generously over French fries smothered with gravy.

Ziti Amin
(1925–2003)
(Ugandan Dictator)

Between 1971-1979, Ziti was just plain overcooked. Many questioned what was in his noodle. He called himself "His Excellency, President for Life, Field Marshal Al Hadji Doctor, Conqueror of the British Empire in African in General and Uganda in Particular". He was always over his head in hot water. Anybody that eccentric must have been hitting the sauce in a big way. Some say he preferred the term "Presidente" because it rhymes with "al dente".

Ronald Oregano
(1911-2004)
(40th President of the United States)

The hero of the Right Wing Republican movement, Oregano served two terms in office (1981-1989). A "B" actor for most of his life, critics wondered how someone with such a spicy name could be so bland. His most famous performance occurred in the 1951 film "Bedtime for Garbonzo," where he delivered a stewing performance. Unfortunately, his film career went from beans to peanuts...convincing him to jump into the political cauldron instead. Served with honor and distinction. And rice.

Tortilla the Hun
(434 – 453 AD)
(Hungarian Invader)

Tortilla ruled the Hunnic Empire in Central Europe. He was an enemy of the Roman Empire who was known for his savagery, brutality, and cruelty. But he was always very kind to corn and flour. His daring exploits made him the taco of the town amongst his countrymen. But his military acumen took an unexpected dip...and the Roman army handed him his head on a tasty platter.

Melon of Troy
(Figure in Greek Mythology)
(Daughter of Zeus)

Known as "The face that launched a thousand ships." When Melon was kidnapped and taken to Troy (modern-day Turkey), 1,000 ships filled with angry Greek soldiers set out to rescue her, resulting in the Trojan War. The famous Trojan Horse story emanates from this tale.

Melon was nearly squashed when her kidnappers rushed her with cucumbers and pickles drawn.

They asked her, "Honeydew"? But she replied, "No. Honey don't". Luckily, they had a change of heart...and she was able to remain seedless. After that, she never went near a guy without her trusty supply of Trojans.

Michelob Gorbachev
(1931--)
(Soviet Leader)

Michelob served from 1985 until the collapse of Soviet communism in 1991. He helped encourage the spread of democracy, which ultimately resulted in the Communist Party of the Soviet Union getting the Schlitz kicked out of them. Through his efforts with U.S. President Ronald Oregano, Michelob helped bring an end to the Cold War; very ironic -- being that everybody enjoys a Cold Michelob. Was awarded the Nobel Peace Prize in 1990. It is said to have commented during his acceptance speech: "I'm proud to be a 'Rooskie'...because it rhymes with 'Brewski'."

Bran Mulroney
(1939 --)
(Canadian Prime Minister)

Bran kept Canada on the crapper from 1984-1993. Bran made many people very irregular by attempting to reform the Constipation. I mean the Constitution. Bran's conservative supporters ("Bran Flakes") finally reached for the plunger in 1993 -- the year that Bran was finally flushed.

Celery Clinton
(1947 --)
(United States Secretary of State, Former First Lady)

Wife of former President of the United States, Bill Clinton. As a result of his well-publicized affair with

Monica Lewinsky, Bill left Celery in a terrible spot. Bill had a bad habit of leaving terrible spots. It seems Bill had a stalk that just wouldn't wilt. Everybody felt sympathy for poor Celery. Everybody, that is, except for that chilled and salt-rimmed, Linda Tripp. Tripp was bloody merry.

Lord Mountbatter

(1900-1979)

(British Admiral, Governor-General of India)

Mountbatter helped India achieve independence from Britain in 1947 by partitioning India into two separate countries: India (Secular), and Pakistan (Muslim). This was carried out with cookie-cutter precision. Some thought that Mountbatter was deflated, but his ideas were really on the rise. Each could taste full independence; but up to this point, they had merely licked the spoon. Mountbatten performed the toothpick test and decided they were done. That really took the cake.

Arnold Schwarzenhamandegger

(1947 --)

(California Governor)

Former actor. Former bodybuilder. Former Austrian. Former ham-and-egger. Since marrying a Kennedy and becoming Governor of California, however, Schwarzenhamandegger now dines on the wealthiest Americans. I mean *with* the wealthiest Americans. Schwarzenhamandegger's muscular physique was the result of years of disciplined weight-training -- as evidenced by his being chosen seven-time "Mr. Steroids". I mean "Mr. Olympia". Schwarzenhamandegger prefers his eggs chopped. When in restaurants, he has been known to yell, "Get to de choppa!" quite aggressively whenever the waiter asks him how he'd like them prepared.

Orchard Nixon

(1913–1994)

(37th President of the United States)

Orchard loved planting things. He had plants everywhere: in the FBI, the CIA, Watergate.... The powers-that-be decided that a thorough pruning was in order, and Orchard was to be impeached. At first, Orchard was excited at the news: he thought “impeachment” meant the planting of more peach trees. David Frost conducted a series of famous interviews with Orchard in 1977. Fortunately for Orchard, there was no lingering Frost damage.

Niacin Mandela
(1918 --)
(President of South Africa)

Niacin was imprisoned for 27 years for being an apartheid activist. This would undoubtedly result in various vitamin deficiencies. He was finally released in 1990, where he immediately set forth on a path that would reenergize his spiritually-malnourished country. From 1994-1999 Niacin served as the President of South Africa -- the first to have ever been democratically elected. Now a healthy and robust 93, he continues to inspire. But not full time. In supplements.

Paunch de León
(1474-1521)
(Spanish Explorer)

Paunch led the first European expedition to Florida in April 1513. He named it "La Florida," due to the abundant vegetation -- and because it was Easter, which the Spaniards called "Pascua Florida" (Festival of Flowers). Legend has it that Paunch went to Florida to discover the magical and elusive Fountain of Youth. Luckily for him, he didn't arrive one month later -- for then he would have been stuck right in the middle of the dreaded March Break.

As it turns out, the "Fountain of Youth" had been a derogatory term used by area natives to describe the thousands upon thousands of exam-weary students who would flock south to enjoy some sand, sun, and frivolity in between term papers. These young people (referred to locally as "those dirty, rotten flockers") would arrive with their parents' blessing aboard a discount fleet of sailing ships known as "The Ramada Armada". This armada consisted of three main ships: "The Visa," "The Master Cardo," and "The Americana Expresso".

Paunch had accidentally found his way to Florida by way of Puerto Rico, the Bahamas, and Cuba -- where Paunch and his sailors stuffed their faces regularly and ate like *animales.* (By the way...Florida puts the "manatee" back in humanity.) It was here that Paunch came to the sad realization that the search for the Fountain of Youth should never begin and end at the refrigerator door.

Gaseous Clay
(1942 --)
(Heavyweight Boxing Champion)

Before changing his name to Muhammad Ali in 1964, Gaseous had already defeated Sonny Liston to claim boxing's ultimate prize. But being from Kentucky, he loved his down-home, southern-fried cooking. The resulting gas and impending diarrhea always kept him one shuffle away from the nearest lavatory. It was also the reason behind his lightning-fast speed in the ring -- for, he was always forced to hurry up and finish a fight lest he shit his trunks and lose by disqualification. ("Float like a butter pie...")

His favorite KO was not Sonny Liston, Joe Frazier, or George Foreman. It was Kaopectate.

Throughout most of his career, Clay/Ali shared a symbiotic relationship with bombastic sports announcer, Howard Cosell. It's a little-known fact that Cosell stumbled upon what would turn out to be his true calling in life while working as a furniture mover. One day, his co-worker accidentally dropped a freezer down a staircase. It just kept rolling and rolling and rolling down the stairs. Cosell was right there, describing the action every step of the way.

He kept repeating: "Down goes freezer! Down goes freezer! Down goes freezer!" The rest is history.

Dwight D. Eisensweetandsour
(1890 – 1969)
(34th President of the United States)

Before becoming president, "Ike" was a five-star general...with a craving for five-star Chinese restaurants. Although hailing from Texas, the Eisensweetandsours were actually early Jehovah's Witnesses. But after converting to Presbyterianism, the only thing Ike would "witness" from then on...were endless take-out containers. Many historians attribute Ike's increasing the number of military personnel into Vietnam in the 1950s to his aching desire to have better access to authentic Chinese cuisine.

Dieting

Many adults get so stressed out over dieting that it keeps them up at night, and often prevents them from getting any sleep. Some of these people are able find relief by drinking a cup of warm milk. Others resort to counting sheep.

The "counting sheep" strategy might not be so effective if you happen to reside in a rough neighborhood like the one I grew up in. That's because every time the sheep would prepare to jump, they'd get shot and killed before they could make it over the fence. Not exactly a "drive-by"...more like a "drive-baaa". High School science class wasn't much better.

They taught us that Einstein's Theory of Relativity was actually "E=MC Hammer". And due to the high incidences of theft which plagued the school, all of the equipment in the lab was strictly hands-off. Whenever one of us would reach for a Bunsen burner, or a test tube, or a beaker...the teacher would yell "You can't touch this!" Then he'd dance around like a moron.

Every morning I'd begin my walk to school by literally stepping over the dead bodies of freshly-killed rappers strewn across our lawn. To this day, I hate it when people throw wrappers on my lawn. Most families of Italian descent, like ours, had a house with a large yard and the obligatory vegetable garden attached. You know what they say about Italians and their big houses: give them an inch...and they'll take the yard.

If I was ever feeling sad or depressed, my mother would try to pick up my spirits up by saying: "Don't worry, son; no matter how dark and hopeless things may appear now, just remember...the sun will always come up tomorrow." There was only one tiny problem with that pearl of wisdom. We lived in the Arctic. The sun wouldn't be up for another six months. (Speaking of the Arctic..."Bipolar" means that someone is Manic Depressive; it does not refer to an Eskimo with homosexual tendencies.)

My eighty-something grandmother happened to be boarding with us during this period. At the best of times, "Nonna" moved slower than a repairman who charges by the hour. But once in the bathroom, you'd think she was reading *War and Peace* in there. Either that, or she was writing a prequel to Stephen King's novel, *The Stand*, to be titled, appropriately, *The Sit.*

My dad was finally compelled to build her a bedroom located closer to the bathroom. That's because Nonna was on an elevated diet of bran and prunes and milk of magnesia.

She would nobly attempt to walk as fast as she could to reach the bathroom in time, but only on rare occasions could she maintain the hard pace necessary to actually make it all the way. The result was never pretty. She was always caught somewhere between a walk and a hard pace. Still, she was my favorite relative, pants down. I mean hands down.

My mother always believed in cooking from scratch. Whenever we ate her food -- it would make the whole family scratch. Mom is now under a court order to not feed the family dog any more table scraps. PETA deemed that it constituted cruelty to animals and threatened to have her arrested. Our dog has never looked better. Even his fleas have more jump. ("I'm going to Frisbeeland!")

My father learned early on in their marriage that Mom was a terrible cook. To get around this, he would secretly tip-toe into the kitchen, then carefully reach back and unplug the oven. And then he'd tell her that it must be broken. Then we'd order out.

We put the die back in "diet"!

There have been countless diets and weight-loss fads which have come and gone over the years. It remains a multi-billion dollar industry. Many opportunistic entrepreneurs have gotten fat off of other people's fat. The concept of "Before & After Pictures" has been etched into our collective psyche like a solid six-pack of abs.

Believe it or not, vegetarianism was considered a fad diet when it was introduced in the mid-1800's. Talk about your "garden variety" diet?

Then, there was "Graham's Bland Diet" back in the 1830's, which tried to steer people away from rich or spicey foods (not to mention tea, coffee, alcohol, meat...and sex). That's also when the Graham Cracker was invented.

In 1912 there was a diet which promised that people would lose weight if they chewed their food exactly 32 times...and then spit it out. Sure you'd lose weight -- that's because you'd literally doze off while doing all that counting and end up not ingesting anything.

The "Vinegar Diet" came about in 1920 and was popularized by the poet Lord Byron. He would douse all of his food in vinegar, which supposedly caused him to lose weight. Needless to say, this diet was very popular among douche bags.

The "Grapefruit Diet" was introduced in the 1920s. Next came the "800 Calorie Diet," which recommended generous portions of grapefruits and coffee. James Cagney must surely have relied on this for inspiration when he squished a grapefruit into Mae Clarke's face in the famous gangster film, *The Public Enemy* (1931). As Moon Zappa, the Valley Girl, would say, "Cagney with a spoon!"

In 1925, Lucky Strike cigarettes decided to jump on the dieting bandwagon. Their new advertising slogan was: "Reach for a Lucky instead of a sweet". You can always count on tobacco companies to have our physical welfare at heart. Their level of sincerity is positively habit-forming; practically addictive! (COUGH! COUGH!)

1928 saw the introduction of the "Inuit Diet," which recommended eating an all-meat-and-fat diet.

1934 saw the advent of the "Bananas and Skim Milk Diet". It remains a huge favorite among overweight monkeys everywhere.

The "Drinking Man's Diet" arrived in 1964. It claimed that you could eat a steak, wash it down with a martini, and still lose weight. That certainly sounds like something only a man could invent!

The "Last Chance Diet" arrived in the 1970s. A more aptly-named diet never existed. That's because it represented the "last chance" for the 58 people who ended up dying a painful death because of it.

The "Atkins Diet" was written in 1972, and became perhaps the most popular diet ever. It was the first of the "high protein-low carbohydrate" diets. It also helped spawn the "South Beach Diet," which espouses low-sugar intake.

The notorious "Scarsdale Diet" followed in 1978, developed by Dr. Herman Tarnower. Barely two short years later in 1980, Dr. Tarnower was shot to death by his long-time lover, Jean Harris. Now *there's* a sure-fire way to lose weight! It not only takes off the pounds -- it *keeps* them off! Ms. Harris is rumored to be working on her own weight loss method. She plans to call it "The Four Bullets At Close Range Diet". (Toe tag and coffin sold separately.) Those were some of the more well known diets.

Now, here are some you may never have heard of: "The Hollywood Cookie Diet," "The Baby Food Diet," "The Hoodia Cactus Plant Diet," "The Blood Type Diet," "The Russian Air Force Diet," "The Chicken Soup Diet," "The Cabbage Soup Diet," "The Acai Berry Diet," "The Negative Calorie Diet," "The 3 Day Diet," "The Bread and Butter Diet," "The Hallelujah Diet," "The Special K Diet," "The Beverly Hills Diet," "The Apple Cider Vinegar Diet," "The Chocolate Diet," "The Peanut Butter Diet," and "The Slimfast Diet".

Do any of these diets really work? Well, they each have their vocal critics who accuse them of being everything from generally unhealthy...to being a flash in the pan...to being voodoo snake-oil mumbo-jumbo...to being downright dangerous. Many people gain the weight right back again. Often more than they lost.

You be the judge. There must be zillions of diet books, plans, methods, and formulas sold every year. Yet there remain zillions of fat people.

Health experts agree that exercise and eating less are still the best strategies available for losing weight. Genetics is also a huge contributing factor. My advice? Try not to have fat parents.

And then, of course, there are those people who have been so heavy for so long that they actually feel guilty for having lost weight ("Forgive me, Father, for I have thinned").

In March, 2011, the laudable Oxford Dictionary announced that it would include 1,000 new words in its lexicon. Many are slang terms such as "LOL," and "OMG". Another is an expression which originated recently in Australia: "Muffin Top". A Muffin Top describes the phenomenon of people (particularly women) who wear pants that are so tight that it causes their fat to hang down over the waistband. It's basically an extension of "love handles".

"Muffin Top" should never be confused with "Carrot Top" -- which describes the phenomena of a guy walking around with his fly unzipped and his erect penis bursting out. (Now that's why I call a *stand-up* comedian!)

Sure-fire signs that you may need to scale back on the snacks a little:

- The Goodfellas refused to whack you because they didn't want to dig a hole that big
- A doorway charged you with assault
- You were assigned your very own drive-thru lane at McDonald's
- Somebody recommended that you really should try Atkins. So you grabbed a knife, a fork, and a bib...and went out looking for anyone named Atkins
- At your job, you specifically asked to work in the department which had the biggest turnover.

The "1-for-1 Reverse-A-Meal" Method

Allow me to unveil my very own groundbreaking weight-loss plan. It's my patented 1-for-1 Reverse-A- Meal method. The 1-for-1 Reverse-A-Meal method is simple and effective. Here's how it works.

First, you'll require two portions of any food item you plan to eat -- whether it be lasagna, banana splits, pizza, hamburgers, fried chicken, cold cut sandwiches, Twinkies, chocolate bars, or donuts. We'll leave that decision totally up to you and your taste buds. Ready?

Good, you can go right ahead and eat portion #1. Finished?

Good. Now here comes the important part. Every time you eat one portion...you shove the other one up your ass. Still with me? Don't talk with your ass full.

My 1-for-1 Reverse-A- Meal method may not be as much fun as "Deal-A-Meal"...but I'll bet Richard Simmons swears by it. Or because of it. It all depends on what he shoved. I mean ate.

But wait -- there's more! You can now own the 1-for-1 Reverse-A-Meal plan for only 16,000 easy payments of $19.99. And if you order now, I'll throw in this lovely decanter (called "The Finger," because it resembles an extended middle finger) -- a regular $40 dollar value -- yours absolutely FREE if you order now!

Oh, and if you decide to return the 1-for-1 Reverse-A-Meal plan? No problem. Keep the finger as my gift to you.

The Bush-Cheney Diet

The Bush-Cheney diet begins and ends with lots of egg...on your face. The Bush-Cheney diet involves lots of chewing and eating; but not of food. How it works is that you chew and eat your way through the national treasury, until you and all of your business associates have become sufficiently well-fattened at the public trough. Why do you think they call it "Pork Barrel" spending anyway? It's because hogs like these are super-greedy pigs, that's why. It's also sometimes referred to as the "Pay Back Your Filthy-Rich Friends Who Got You There" diet.

Skeptics might call it "looting" -- but a "Loot Bag" implies something that's fun for children at Halloween (Osama Bin Goblin?).

Sneaking snacks in between meals is strictly forbidden; but stealing an election or two is perfectly alright if you think you can get away with it.

(IMPORTANT DISCLAIMER: Do NOT become discouraged if you see people around you dropping like flies as a result of starvation. That's their problem. To help out your neighbors would constitute the first step towards Socialism. Let the unlucky losers find their own country to plunder.)

Don't believe what the so-called experts say about exercise, either. It's much better to just go hide away on "vacation" at your ranch for at least a full one third of the year. You'll see the pounds begin to melt away soon enough as a result of all the telephoning you have ahead of you: your many private contractor buddies will need to be notified that you just enabled them to suck up endless billions of tax payer dollars by creating two phony wars. You see, this diet is unique in that it believes in spreading the fat around.

Some people call them "leftovers". Others prefer the term "surplus". Either way, if George W. Bush proved one thing, it was this: before you go out and buy a ton of groceries, it's wiser to first go through any supplies you may already have on hand. Luckily for George W. Bush and Dick Cheney, Bill Clinton had kept the shelves well stocked in the White House upon his exit. In fact, Paul McCartney is thinking of releasing a new version of "Hello, Goodbye," and dedicating it to George W. Bush. It will be called "Hello Surplus...Goodbye Surplus".

"As your President, I will not rest until the world is one giant, polluted, smoking crater...that smells like burning tires."

Do you know why Rose and Valerie were screaming from the gallery? It's because Dick Cheney had just let out their secret true identities as undercover CIA agents.

McCartney also plans to re-work other popular Beatles hits -- such as "I Don't Want To Spoil The Party (But I Just Ruined The Republican Party)," "With A Little Help From My Friends At Halliburton," and a souped-up version of "Baby You Can Drive My Car," entitled "Baby You Can Drive My Country Into The Ground".

Now, I don't know about you, but I always got the impression that Bush must have had a craving for smoked meats. Why do I say that? Well, we all remember Bush saying how he was "gonna smoke 'em out of their caves and bring 'em to justice" over and over and over again in his "press conferences," right? What, exactly, was he referring to? Ham? Salmon? Turkey? What meats did he intend to smoke?

Speaking of turkeys, Bush seems to have had suddenly and inexplicably lost his craving for smoked meats early on in his "war against terror". I mean, his sudden change of appetite was certainly fortunate for his quarry, because *that* famous turkey ended up escaping, and was conspicuously never spoken of again by Bush (Osama Been Gobble-Gobble-Gobblin'?*)*. Was all that "smoke" talk merely a smoke screen all along? Is it possible that George never *really* liked smoked meats? Was "the turkey" merely a decoy who was permitted to duck without even causing a flap?

Somewhere along the line, George developed a taste for lox. As a matter of fact, some of his friends suggested he should keep lox in his refrigerator. But George being George, he misunderstood what they meant...and went and put a lock on the refrigerator door instead. The poor man: he ended up almost starving to death before eventually remembering the combination. That's because he kept it written down on the last place he'd ever have the stomach to look: the mirror.

Outraged voters have no right to act surprised that Bush and Cheney turned out to be such rotten eggs. After all, you get what you deserve if you go and place weasels in charge of a hen house. It's no coincidence that Bush appealed to local folks who were yokels. That's because if you combine "yolks," "folks," and "locals"...you get "yokels".

This diet is extremely devastating to the system (not to mention the economy, the environment, and anyone who makes less than $5,000,000 a year), so it's not recommended you stay on it for more than two consecutive four-year periods (or "terms").

It's also highly advisable that you begin each and every morning with a rigorous constitutional. That's because there isn't much of the Constitution left...so you'd better enjoy it while you can.

The Bush-Cheney diet is specially formulated to appeal to oil, credit, insurance, and pharmaceutical companies, Wall Street, weapons manufacturers, the military, banks, and special interest groups. In fact, the designers of this plan went all out to make sure it was as deregulated as possible so that all of these entities could benefit from the unobstructed bounty that lay ahead of them.

The cost of the Bush-Cheney Diet Plan is what it is. There are no discounts. It cannot be negotiated. You must pay full retail price plus tax. Well, not entirely...they do offer tax cuts to the richest 1%!

Food On Radio

Before television... there was radio. Radio was where it's at. Practically every old-time performer you've ever heard of got their start there. Radio was largely an extension of Vaudeville. And practically every old-time performer you've ever heard of got their start there -- including Al Jolson, W.C. Fields, Buster Keaton, the Marx Brothers, Jimmy Durante, Bill "Bojangles" Robinson, Jackie Gleason, Fanny Brice, Harry Houdini, Eddie Cantor, Kate Smith, Milton Berle, Judy Garland, Bob Hope, Bing Crosby, Rose Marie, Sammy Davis Jr., Red Skelton, Burns and Allen, and the Three Stooges.

Vaudeville offered entertainment-hungry patrons a variety-based format featuring acts ranging from singing, dancing, comedy, magic, animals, acrobats, jugglers, and one-act scenes from famous plays; sort of like a traveling *Ed Sullivan Show*. Vaudeville acts toured theater halls, clubs, and auditoriums throughout the United States and Canada from the early 1880s until the early 1930s. But then along came movies and radio. Theater owners soon realized that it was much cheaper for them to rent and screen movies -- especially the recently-invented "talkies".

Less overhead, too; and I'm not just referring to the drunken acrobats they had to worry about swinging above their heads. But mainly, there were much bigger profits to be had.

Toronto is now the third largest theater market in the world -- after New York, and London. Today, The Elgin and Winter Garden Theaters in Toronto house the world's largest collection of vaudeville props and scenery. They are the last surviving Edwardian stacked theaters in the world. "Stacked" means they are built one on top of another. It doesn't mean they've got huge boobs for customers.

During the time of vaudeville, they were called "Loew's Yonge Street Theater". When vaudeville finally died, they were boarded up for decades, leaving a treasure trove of artifacts within their hallowed halls just waiting to be rediscovered.

Through the miracle of sponsorships, food would play an instrumental role in the supporting, developing, and maintaining of some of our most beloved institutions, in an entertainment industry that was still in its infancy. Food got them to the big leagues. Food kept them there. Food would allow them to simmer away on the front burners until television was finally ready to emerge from the dugout and approach the empty plate to advance the runner.

Not even the "Say Hey Kid" himself, Willie Mayonnaise, could have done it with any more zip. (Neither could "Slammin'" Sammy Samosa.)

Jack Benny began on radio in 1932. But it wasn't called *The Jack Benny Show*. It was called *The Canada Dry Program.* Benny would stay on radio and television for more than thirty years, until 1965.

After switching networks (and sponsors), his show then became known as *The Jell-O Program Starring Jack Benny.* When sugar became scarce due to the rationing during World War II, it then became *The Grape Nuts Program Starring Jack Benny.* This should not be confused with *The Numb Nuts Program Starring George W. Bush.* Yet another sponsor from his long-running television show was Lipton Tea.

Little Orphan Annie was a popular radio show for children which ran from 1930 to 1940. It was sponsored by Ovaltine. Ovaltine dropped out in 1940, and from 1940 until 1942, the show was sponsored by Quaker Puffed Wheat Sparkies. Remember how in the movie *A Christmas Story* (1983), the lead character "Ralphie" fortified himself in the bathroom in a desperate attempt to crack the code with his secret decoder ring? Well, in fact, no such rings were ever produced by Ovaltine.

Most deciphering devices for kids were either pins or badges and were either included in breakfast cereals or Cracker Jack as prizes, or could be sent away for with a box top or label as proof of purchase. The message, "Be sure to drink your Ovaltine," was never transmitted during any of the show's broadcasts. This was simply dreamed up by author Jean Shepherd, author of *In God We Trust, All Others Pay Cash* (1966) -- the book on which the movie *A Christmas Story* was based. In hindsight, I'm sure Shepherd knew what he was doing, being that this was one of the most charming parts of the movie.

General Mills has remained a top producer of food products since 1856. Their stable of goodies includes Cheerios, Chex, Boo Berry, Cocoa Puffs, Count Chocula, Franken Berry, Trix, Wheaties, Betty Crocker, Bisquick, Pillsbury, Fruit Roll-Ups, Bugles, Haagen Dazs, Betty Crocker, Green Giant, Hamburger Helper, and Yoplait.

It was General Mills that was the sponsor for the legendary radio and television show, *The Lone Ranger*, which ran from 1941 to 1961 ("Hi-yo, Silver...away!"). In 1959, General Mills also sponsored the *Rocky and His Friends* television show, which later prompted *The Bullwinkle Show.* Red Skelton would later consider suing the actor who provided the voice of Bullwinkle, claiming he had lifted it from his own "Clem Kadiddlehopper". He ended up not suing.

In the 1930s Rudy Vallee could be heard warbling through his megaphone on *The Fleischmann's Yeast Hour* -- where George Burns and Gracie Allen would make their American radio debut in 1932 (George went West...Gracie went Yeast). In 1936, the two got their very own show, but it would not be called *The Burns and Allen Show.* Instead, it was called *The Maxwell House Coffee Time.* Maxwell House became famous for their slogan "Good to the last drop," which they introduced in 1917. However, the term is strongly believed to have been uttered by President Theodore Roosevelt.

One thing *is* for sure: Coca-Cola used the slogan "Good to the last drop" in 1907 -- before either of them. As it turns out, Coke is the real thing after all!

This is how each episode of *The Maxwell House Coffee Time* would begin:

Gracie: Another cup of Maxwell House coffee, George?
George: Sure. Pour me a cup, Gracie.
Gracie: You know, Maxwell House is always good to the last...drop.
George: And that drop's good, too.

The notorious "War of the Worlds" with Orson Welles was broadcast as part of *The Mercury Theater On The Air* radio show in 1938. Although the show had been struggling with low ratings, the success of "War of the Worlds" convinced Campbell's Soup to become their new sponsor, thus ensuring the show's continued survival. The show's name was soon changed to *The Campbell Playhouse.* (I wonder if instead of yelling "Action!" the director would yell "Soup's On!"?)

In 1937, Edgar Bergen and Charlie McCArthy were given their own radio show. But it would not be called *The Edgar Bergen and Charlie McCarthy Show.* It was called *The Chase And Sanborn Hour.* Apparently, Chase and Sanborn Coffee had so much caffeine in it back then that it could even make an otherwise stiff, wooden dummy talk. I'm referring to Charlie McCarthy...not Ronald Reagan.

During the World War II years, *The Adventures of Superman* was a hugely successful radio serial. It was sponsored by Kellog's Pep cereal. Pep was soon discontinued, but the company still makes All-Bran, Apple Jacks, Bran Flakes, Cocoa Krispies, Corn Flakes, Corn Pops, Eggo, Fruit Loops, Frosted Flakes, Frosted Min-Wheats, Honey Smacks, Mueslix, Raisin Bran, Rice Krispies, and Special K. (From serial. To cereal. To no more serial. Very surreal.)

A versatile performer in movies and clubs, comic actor Danny Kaye was lured into radio with *The Danny Kaye Show (sponsored by Pabst Blue Ribbon).* Can you guess who the sponsor was? Although the show lasted only two years (1945-1956), it cemented his position as a blue ribbon entertainer.

Before *I Love Lucy* was *I Love Lucy* on television...it was *My Favorite Husband* on radio. It ran from 1948 through 1951 and was sponsored by Jello-O. Here is how each weekly episode would begin:

Announcer: It's time for My Favorite Husband starring Lucille Ball!
Lucille Ball: Jell-O, everybody!
Announcer: Yes, it's the gay family comedy series starring Lucille Ball with Richard Denning and is brought to you by the Jell-O family of Red-Letter Desserts.
Singers: J-E-L-L-
O! The big red letters stand for the Jell-O family,
Oh, the big red letters stand for the Jell-O family,
That's Jell-O!
Yum, yum, yum!
Jell-O pudding!
Yum, yum, yum!
Jell-O tapioca pudding, yes sir-ee!
Announcer: Now, let's take a look at the Cooper family, two people who live together and like it.

Wow...they sure don't write them like that anymore, do they? I don't know what's more precious -- Lucille Ball saying "Jell-O, everybody!", or the show being described as "...the gay family comedy series". Yum, yum, yum! Yes sir-ee! Why, golly gee-whiz. People sure were corny back then!

Lucille Ball was encouraged to do a television version of the show but insisted that her real-life husband Desi Arnaz play her on-screen husband. That's how *I Love Lucy* was born. This revolutionizer of situation comedies would go on to dominate television from 1951 to 1957.

Food On Television

After radio...there was television. Television had a distinct advantage over radio in that it had the luxury of combining sound with pictures. It was a feast for the senses. In the days of radio, you would literally stare at the radio (or your feet) while listening to your favorite program. You were forced to rely completely on your imagination to help conjure up what was unfolding in the script.

But with television, the action was laid out right there in front of you -- clear as a bell pepper. Well, not quite; early TVs were nothing if not grainy, hissy, and out of focus. Still, regardless how bad the picture quality was, you could now see little people walking across your TV screen. You'd *never* see little people walking across your radio (or feet) -- not unless you'd experienced a serious brain injury, or suffered from some sort of a psychiatric disorder. Or were insane. Or just plain cuckoo-for-cocoa puffs.

Even music -- the traditional bread-and-butter staple of radio -- was given a new dimension. Now, you could actually *see* the band playing your favorite songs, while immaculately-dressed people danced to them.

Although televisions first came into use in the late-1920s, they wouldn't become widespread or affordable until the 1940s, with the advent of networks. The Dumont Television Network debuted in 1946, NBC began in 1947, and both CBS and ABC arrived in 1948. In Canada, the CBC commenced sucking up public tax dollars in 1952.

"And now, a word from our sponsors"

The glorious period between the late 1940s and 1961 is what's widely considered to be "The Golden Age of

Television". That's interesting -- since the programs were broadcast and viewed in black-and-white.

As with radio before it, television would benefit greatly by having many of its programs sponsored by food companies. Having a solid company with reliable financial resources behind your show could make all the difference between being a "hit" or a "miss". (By that, I don't mean *Our Miss Brooks* (1952-1956). True, she was a Miss...but the show was definitely a hit.) On the other hand, having a fly-by-night sponsor, or one which offered a limited budget, would be reflected in poor production values, sets, and caliber of guest stars. If that happened...you'd be steamed.

In1949, *The Goldbergs* moved to television after a successful run on Broadway. The program ran a successful seven seasons until its cancellation in 1955. The show's original sponsor was Sanka Coffee. It was enough to keep you up at night. The show, I mean...not the coffee.

By 1949 the folksy Arthur (The Ukulele Man) Godfrey was already a long-time veteran of radio. In short order, Godfrey would be hosting *three* successful shows on television: *Arthur Godfrey's Talent Scouts* (1948), *Arthur Godfrey and His Friends* (1949), and *Arthur Godfrey Time* (1952). Among his sponsors were Lipton Tea, and Pillsbury. The second of these shows -- the informal weekly program known as *Arthur Godfrey and His Friends* -- turned out to be the most successful, running until 1957.

But it was *Arthur Godfrey's Talent Scouts* which gave newcomer Steve Allen his first big break. Allen had been called in as a last-minute replacement for Godfrey. He went on to make an unforgettable and lasting impression with viewers by demonstrating Godfrey's two sponsor products (Lipton Tea, and soap) by mixing them together in Godfrey's unsuspecting ukulele. Allen would soon create his own program in 1954, which would come to be known as...*The Tonight Show.*

Luckily for Steve, Jay Leno was barely four years old at the time. This meant he wouldn't be able to steal the show away from him no matter how hard he tried.

The Burns and Allen Show began in 1950, and was an immediate success. It would enjoy a successful run which would not evaporate until 1958. The program was sponsored by Carnation. George and Gracie wore their success proudly on their sleeves...and their lapels.

Roy Rogers and Dale Evans were one of America's best-known and most-beloved couples. Roy Rogers (born Leonard Franklin Slye) was a singer and an actor. He made his first film in 1935, and would end up appearing in a total of 100 features throughout his remarkable career. Dale Evans (born Lucille Wood Smith) was a singer and a songwriter who made her debut film performance in 1942.

Their first movie together was released in 1946. In 1947, they formally hitched their wagons and tied the slipknot. That's Western talk meaning they were married.

Their popularity as a couple was so immediate and so resounding that it resulted in their very own television series, *The Roy Rogers Show*. The show spawned 100 episodes, from 1951 until 1957, and introduced the world to their magnificent horse, Trigger, and their German Sheppard wonder dog, Bullet. Fortunately for their future children, Roy and Dale would ditch the gun metaphors when it came time to naming their offspring. Having to put up with "Chamber," "Barrel," "Firing Pin," "Hammer," and "Magazine" all crawling around the ranch in diapers would have been a bit much.

The Roy Rogers Show was sponsored by the Post Cereals arm of General Foods. Well-known Post cereals include Alpha-Bits, Cocoa Pebbles, Grape Nuts, Honeycomb, Shredded Wheat, Shreddies, and Sugar Crisp.

The Red Skelton Show enjoyed a phenomenal 20-year run, from 1951 to 1971. Skelton's list of comical characters included, "Sheriff Deadeye," "San Fernando Red," "Cauliflower McPugg," "Clem Kadiddlehopper," and "Freddie the Freeloader". In 1965, The Rolling Stones would make their American television debut on *The Red*

Skelton Show. Skelton was well known for his closing tag-line, "Good night, and may God bless".

One of Red's sponsors was the PET Milk Company -- the first evaporated milk available on the market. Evaporated milk was very sought after during this era because very few people owned refrigerators.

Even fewer people knew what the hell to make of Keith Richards.

Geritol is an iron and b-vitamin supplement. It mainly sponsored shows which were directed at somewhat *older* audiences.

For example: *What's My Line* was the longest running prime-time game show in American television history. From 1950 to 1967, it appeared weekly but then continued on as a daily show from 1968 to 1978. The premise was simple: a contestant would appear before a panel of celebrities who would ask a limited number of questions in an effort to try and guess the person's identity or occupation. If the panel guessed correctly, the contestant would be blindfolded and then shot. Ok, I made up that last part.

Ted Mack's Original Amateur Hour ran from 1948 until 1954. It served as the predecessor of such shows as *Star Search, The Gong Show,* and *America's Got Talent.*

The Lawrence Welk Show (1955-1971) was a long-running variety show staple. Every week, Lawrence would conduct a big band while blue-haired audience members attempted to dance along to a selection of "Champagne Favorites"...without dropping their dentures. ("And now, please-a welcome, Bobby-uh, and Sissy-uh!")

Twenty-One (1956-1958) was the game show accused of providing players with the correct answers to help boost ratings. This resulted in the famous quiz show scandal which spurred a Senate investigation into corruption, and very nearly resulted in the removal of all quiz shows from the air. The scandal became the basis for the movie, *Quiz Show* (1994), starring Robert Redford.

Hee Haw (1969-1992) provided viewers with an idealized depiction of American rednecks, hillbillies, and bumpkins -- complete with banjo music, denim overalls, and jug whiskey. The kicker? Two of the series' three creators were Canadian, and the show was produced by a company called Yongestreet Productions. Yonge Street runs directly through Toronto, and, until very recently, was listed in the Guinness Book of Records as the world's longest street. ("SAA-LUTE!")

During its first three seasons, *The Danny Thomas Show* was actually called *Make Room For Daddy.* Most people, however, immediately took to calling it *The Danny Thomas Show*...because it starred a guy named "Danny Thomas"...and Danny Thomas had a show...so the name was changed to *The Danny Thomas Show.* The show enjoyed a very strong nine- year run from, from 1953 to 1964. At various times, Danny's sponsors included Post Cereals, Jell-O, and Maxwell House.

Kraft Music Hall moved from radio to television in 1958. The show's longest-serving and most popular host was Perry Como, but other guest hosts included Milton Berle, Rock Hudson, Lorne Greene, George Burns, Dinah Shore, Ed McMahon, and Woody Allen. The show lasted until 1971, and featured the cream of the crop of the entertainment world. (Note: Contrary to popular rumors, Perry was not related to Donald Trump. His name was "Perry Como"...not "Perry Comb-Over".)

Kraft Suspense Theater ran from 1963 to 1965, and was alternated with the monthly *Kraft Music Hall. Kraft Suspense Theater* was one of the few suspense series telecast in color at the time. Color TV would not become widespread until 1965. To this very day, many stores in the southern United States still have signs up that read, "No Coloreds Allowed" -- and they even employ white-hooded men to ride around on horseback to enforce that position. But let's not get go there...it's most unpalatable.

Pete and Gladys (1960-1962) was a situation comedy starring Harry Morgan ("Col. Potter" from *M*A*S*H*). The modest hit was a variation of *I Love Lucy* (complete with wacky red-headed wife). As a matter of fact, *Pete and Gladys* was produced during the two-year period between the end of *The Luci-Desi Comedy Hour*, and the beginning of *The Lucy Show*, and even featured regular appearances by Gale Gordon ("Mr. Mooney" from *The Lucy Show*). Morgan would remain optimistic as he witnessed his career go from pot…to Potter. Sponsors included Kellogg's, and Carnation.

The Twilight Zone was a groundbreaking science fiction anthology series created by Rod Serling. Every week from 1959 to 1964 Serling reminded viewers that they had just entered into a dimension of sound, sight, and mind. They had also entered into a dimension of Minute Rice, Jell-O, Log Cabin Syrup, Hellman's Mayonnaise, Sanka, Maxwell House, and Birdseye: all best-selling products of the show's sponsor, General Foods.

"We're having pork chopsh, and appleshauce. Isn't that schwell?"

Food is at the heart of some of the most hilarious and memorable scenes ever depicted on television. Ditto with many of our most often-uttered catchphrases.

Here are some notable reruns. Just like food likes to repeat itself on you…so do TV shows.

I Love Lucy

"Switching Jobs" (1952)

Lucy and Ethel decide to supplement their incomes, so they take a job working in a chocolate factory. Their task is to wrap individual chocolates that travel by them on a conveyor belt. The assignment begins easily enough. But then the conveyor belt begins to speed up.

Then it speeds up some more. Finally, the girls simply can't keep up with the chocolates, which are now whizzing by them.

To compensate, Lucy and Ethel are forced to scoop up handfuls of the chocolates, which they shove down the fronts of their dresses, in their mouths, under their hats....wherever they can fit them. It was pure chocolate mayhem.

"Lucy Does a TV Commercial" (1952)

Lucy acts as product spokesperson on one of Ricky's specials. It's her job to pitch a vitamin tonic called, "Vitameatavegamin" -- a concoction containing vitamins, meat, vegetables, and minerals. Unfortunately, the director needs her to perform take after take of the commercial, and every time she finishes a re-take she is then required to drink another teaspoonful of the ghastly-tasting liquid. What Lucy doesn't realize is that the tonic contains 23% alcohol, which succeeds in leaving her good and smashed by the end of the routine. In reality, the bottle was filled with apple pectin.

"Pioneer Women" (1952)

Lucy and Ethel bet Desi and Fred $50 that they can live without modern conveniences. The one exception is an oven. Next, Lucy decides to make home-made bread, but adds 13 cloves of yeast instead of the required three. The result is an 18-foot loaf of bread that springs out of the oven and pins her against the sink.

"Lucy Does the Tango" (1957)

Lucy and Ethel stuff their shirts and pants with as many whole eggs as they can fit. They were bound to get broken. This episode features the longest-ever recorded laugh for a television series (65 seconds). (Note: In 1965 NBC premiered its popular musical-variety series, *Hullabaloo*, to compete with the highly-successful, *Shindig!*, and *American Bandstand*. For a time, they considered combining *Hullabalo* with *Here's Lucy*, and calling it *HullabaLucy*. But network executives feared it would result in too many HullabaLucynations.)

Bewitched
"Samantha's Power Failure" (1969)

Samantha is stripped of her powers by the Witches Council. Because Cousin Serena and Uncle Arthur publically supported her in her position, they too end up getting their powers removed as punishment. The two decide that if Samantha can live like a mortal without powers, then so can the two of them. They end up working in an ice-cream parlor where it is their job to dip bananas in chocolate sauce, roll them in chopped nuts, and put them in a tray.

This episode of *Bewitched* is a reworking of the *I Love Lucy* episode "Switching Jobs". As with the *Lucy* episode, the conveyor belt transporting the bananas begins to speed up so fast that Serena and Arthur can't possibly keep up with them. "Uncle Arthur" (Paul Lynde) chips in plenty of sarcasm and one-liners ("How unskilled do you think we are?"). The scene ends in a chocolate sauce fight with the restaurant's antagonistic manager.

Both episodes were directed by Elizabeth Montgomery's then-husband, William Asher. "Cousin Serena" is actually Elizabeth Montgomery in a dual role.

The Beverly Hillbillies
(1962-1971)

For ten riotous seasons, Granny Clampett loved nothing better than to feed both strangers and kin folk alike generous portions of her scrumptious down-home vittles, including hog jowls and possum belly. But if the strange food ever caused somebody's throat to spring a leak and begin to eject vomit like a gushing BP oil well leak, then either Ellie May, Jethro, or Uncle Jed would invariably yell, "Granny...clamp it!"

Monty Python's Flying Circus
"Spam" (1970)

Two customers ("Mr. And Mrs. Bun" -- played by Eric Idle and Graham Chapman) are trying to order breakfast from a menu that includes Spam in practically every dish. ("Spam, Spam, Spam, Spam, Spam, Spam, baked beans, Spam, Spam, and Spam.") Regrettably for Mrs. Bun, she is the only person in the room who does not like spam.

The Brady Bunch
"The Personality Kid" (1971)

Peter Brady attends a party where he is told that he has no personality. He tries to remedy the situation by going about inventing a new personality for himself. He does this by impersonating Humphrey Bogart: "We're having pork chopsh and appleshauche." Florence Henderson would add the "Isn't that schwell?" part later in the episode...because she had an over-abundance of Wessonality.

The Odd Couple
"Sleepwalker" (1971)

Oscar makes a real effort to try and be nicer to Felix. Unfortunately, Felix's annoying nit-picking and perfectionism only serves to make Oscar even crazier. As a way of coping, he begins to sleepwalk. Oscar's nightly unrest leads him directly to Felix's room, where he swats a sleeping Felix over the head with a rolled up newspaper. ("I don't like pits, pits, pits, in my juice, juice, juice!")

The Mary Tyler Moore Show
(1970-1977)

The character "Sue Ann Nivens" (Betty White) first appeared on the show in 1973. Sue Ann was the host of a woman's show carried on Mary's station called *The Happy Homemaker*. Sue Ann was at various times competitive, sarcastic, nasty, and sex-starved; very often, all at the same time.

Saturday Night Live
(1975--)

Many of this long-running sketch show's most all-time popular skits involved food. "Samurai Delicatessen" starred John Belushi. Belushi would prepare your favirute deli sandwich using traditional samurai cutting methods. The sketch was written by Don Novello ("Father Guido Sarducci").

"Super Bass-O-Matic '76" featured a frantic Dan Ackroyd as a Paul Popeil-type infomercial announcer trying to up-sell a blender which turns raw bass into bass paste. ("Wow, that's terrific bass!")

"Little Chocolate Donuts" featured John Belushi spoofing both Wheaties cereal and Olympian, Bruce Jenner. At the end, Marv Albert says "Little Chocolate Donuts. The Donuts of Champions!"

"Olympia Cafe" starred John Belushi, Bill Murray, Dan Ackroyd, and Larraine Newman as harried ethnic workers in a greasy spoon restaurant. ("Cheeburgeh, cheeburgeh, cheep, cheep! No Coke -- Pepsi.")

"Hub's Gyros" featured the catchphrase, "You like-a da juice, ah?". Apparently, customers just couldn't get enough of that delicious gyros juice. The sketch starred Rob Schneider, Adam Sandler, Mike Myers, David Spade, Chris Farley, and Tim Meadows.

The Muppet Show
(1976-1981)

"The Swedish Chef" loves to wave his utensils in the air like a medieval mace, while singing his trademark song which always ends in "Bôrk, bôrk, bôrk!". Specialty dishes include: "Salad ala Boom-Boom," "Lobster Bandidos," "Meat Loafers," and "Squirrel Stew".

Seinfeld

"The Soup Nazi" (1995)

Jerry and the gang discover a local food nook which makes fantastic soup. The problem now is that the hot-tempered head chef is a very stiff and regimented sort who demands that his customers comport themselves in a particular manner. If they don't, he will cut them off and deny them food by yelling "No soup for you!"

Television series would sometimes insert a maid or a cook or a butler into the cast, very often as a reliable vehicle for timely comic delivery. They included "Hop Sing" from *Bonanza* (Victor Sen Yung), "Uncle Charlie" from My Three Sons (William Demarest), "Mr. French" from *Family Affair* (Sebasten Cabot), "Alice" from *The Brady Bunch* (Ann B. Davis), "Mildred" from *Macmillan and Wife* (Nancy Walker), "Benson" from *Soap* (Robert Guilluame), "Florence" from *The Jeffersons* (Marla Gibbs), and "Tony" from *Who's the Boss?* (Tony Danza).

Other series would install eating or drinking establishments around which the plot would revolve. These include "Kelsey's Bar," and "Archie Bunker's Place" from All In The Family; "Arnold's Drive-In," from Happy Days; "The Pizza Bowl," from Laverne & Shirley; "Mel's Diner," from Alice; "The Regal Beagle," from Three's Company; "Danny's" from Quincy M.E.; "Cheers," from Cheers; "Moe's Tavern," and "Kiwk-E-Mart" from The Simpsons; "Monk's Café," from Seinfeld; "Nemo's Restaurant," from Everybody Loves Raymond; "The Drunken Clam," from Family Guy; and even The Soprano's -- which boasted four: the "Bada-Bing," "Satriale's Pork Store," "Crazy Horse," and "Vesuvio".

Still other characters conjured up an instant association with a particular favorite food or beverage. "Kojak" lived for lollipos, "Columbo" loved his chili, "Hawkeye" from *M*A*S*H* insisted on his martinis, the Golden Girls would work out their problems over a cheesecake...and Bob and Doug McKenzie guzzled lots and lots of beer, eh?

Mascots

Food products have given birth to a multitude of spokespeople -- animated, and otherwise. Many of these remain some of the most cherished and well-known characters in popular culture.

For Food:

"Miss Chuiquita" from the Chiquita Bananas
"Peter Pan" for Peter Pan peanut butter
The Kraft Macaroni and Cheese Dinosaur, "Cheesasaurus Rex"
The "Otter Pops"
"Captain Cupcake," "Fruit Pie the Magician," and "Twinkie the Kid" -- all three from Hostess products
"Willie Wonka's Nerds"
"The Campbell's Soup Kids"
"Mr. Salty" the Pretzel Man
Hamburger Helper's "Helping Hand"
"Charlie the Tuna" for Starkist
"The M&M's"
"The California Raisins"
"The Jolly Green Giant" and "Sprout"
"Aunt Jemina"
"The Arby's Oven Mitt"
"Betty Crocker"
"Mr. Owl" for Tootsie Pops
"Uncle Ben"
"Willie Wonka" for the Willie Wonka Candy Company
"Wendy" for Wendy's
"Floyd D. Duck" for Bubble Yum
"The Klondike Bar Polar Bear"
"Dairy Fairy" for Kraft Cheese Slices
"Chef Boyardee"
"The Chicken of the Sea Mermaid"
"Sailor Jack and his dog, Bingo" for Crackerjack

"Duncan Hines"
"The Morton Salt Girl"
"Milton the Toaster" for Pop Tarts
"Popsicle Pete"
"Fred the Baker" for Dunkin' Donuts
"Frito Bandito" for Frito-Lay
"W.C. Fritos" for Frito-Lay
"Harvey" for Harvey's
"Mother Nature" for Chiffon Margarine
"Gidget the Chihuahua" for Taco Bell
"Noid" for Domino's Pizza
"Hamm's Beer Bear" for Hamm's Beer
"The Gerber Baby"
"The Snack Fairy" for Fig Newtons
The "Vlasic Stork"
"Speedy Alka Seltzer"
The Mrs. Butterworth's talking syrup bottle
"Mr. Peanut" for Planters
"Ronald McDonald"
"The Burger King"
"The Keebler Elves"
"Chester Cheetah" for Cheetohs
and The Pillsbury Doughboy himself, "Poppin' Fresh".

For Cereal:
"The Apple Jacks"
"Count Chocula"
"Frankenberry"
"Boo Berry"
"Quisp" and "Quake" from Quaker Oats
"Snap, Crackle, and Pop"
"The Trix Rabbit"
"The Quaker Oats Man"
"Tony the Tiger"
"Lucky the Leprechaun" for Lucky Charms
"The Dig'em Frog" for Sugar Smacks
"Toucan Sam" for Fruit Loops
"Cap'n Crunch"
"Sonny" the Cuckoo-for-Cocoa Puffs Cuckoo Bird

"Buzz Bee" the Honey Nut Cheerios Bee
"Sunny" the Raisin Bran Sun
"Sugar Bear" -- first of Sugar Crisp, now of Super Golden Crisp
and "Mikey" from Life Cereal ("He likes everything").

For Beverages:
"The Budweiser Alligator"
"The Budweiser Frogs"
"Spuds Mackenzie" for Anheuser Busch Beer
"The Icee Polar Bear"
"Cora the Coffee Lady" for Maxwell House
The A&W "Great Root Bear" and "Rosie Bear"
The 7up "Cool Spot"
"Quicky" the Nesquick Bunny
"The Coca Cola Polar Bears"
"Punchy" for Hawaiian Punch
and the "Pitcher Man" for Koolaid.

Honorable Mentions:
"The Fruit of the Loom Guys" - No, they didn't advertise food...but their legend looms small, large, and extra-large.
"Jiffy Pop Popcorn" - Grown-ups would always tell us not play with our food...only to turn around and buy us this stuff...that they would then encourage us to play with!
"Dog the Bounty Hunter" - Not only does Dog track down dangerous fugitives...he's also the Quicker Picker Upper.

Bubble Gum Cards

Thin sticks of bright pink chewing gum first began appearing in trading cards in the 1951 Topps baseball series. (Before that, each pack came with a single cigarette!) The practice was largely abandoned in 1992 when collectors complained that it was damaging the potentially-valuable cargo. (A mint condition 1952 Mickey Mantle could today fetch upwards of $80,000 on the open market -- but maybe only one quarter of that amount if "The Mick" happened to be sporting a big wad of gum crud stuck to his face.)

While trading cards had traditionally catered to sports fans (such as baseball, hockey, basketball, football, and boxing), bubble gum cards would go on to achieve even greater popularity by tapping into the ever-burgeoning television landscape.

1950s:

Hopalong Cassidy, Davy Crockett, Roy Rogers, Gunsmoke, Robin Hood, TV Western Stars, Television and Radio Stars of N.B.C., Three Stooges, Uncle Miltie.

1960s:

Adventures of Rin Tin Tin, Superman, Batman, The Adams Family, The Beverley Hillbillies, The Avengers, The Beatles, Combat!, Casper, Dark Shadows, Get Smart, Gilligan's Island, Gomer Pyle, Green Berets, Daktari, Land of the Giants, The Green Hornet, Hogan's Heroes, Laugh-In, Lost In Space, The Man From U.N.C.L.E., Danger Man/Secret Agent, The Munsters, The Mod Squad, The Monkees, Tarzan, The High Chaparral, McHale's Navy, The Outer Limits, Rat Patrol, Star Trek, Voyage to the Bottom of the Sea.

1970s:

Battlestar Galactica, Bionic Woman, Buck Rodgers, Charlie's Angels, Good Times, The Jackson 5, The Osmonds, Happy Days, The Incredible Hulk, Kung Fu, Mork & Mindy, The Partridge Family, Ripley's Believe It Or Not, The Six Million Dollar Man, Space:1999, Three's Company, Welcome Back Kotter, Super Heroes, Planet of the Apes, Elvis, CHiPS.

1980s:

Garbage Pail Kids, WWF (World Wrestling Federation), Go-Bots, Cyndi Lauper, Growing Pains, Harry and the Hendersons, Pee-Wee's Playhouse, Max Headroom.

Kids could now be seen at home or in schoolyards everywhere indulging in such games of skill and precision as “Closies,” “Knocksies,” or “Flipsies”. The much-dreaded “Scrambles!” was usually inflicted on a kid you didn’t much like. You’d wait for him to pick up his deck of cards...then you’d smack them out of his hands with a forceful upward motion when he wasn’t looking. Then you’d belt out the obligatory “Scrambles!”.

The result would be an exploding mushroom cloud of bubble gum cards raining down over everyone’s head; like a ticker-tape parade for midgets.

Next, all you’d see would be mere flashes of dozens of frantic kids swooping in to pick off cards from all directions like ravenous hyenas, while the stunned victim would stand helplessly by watching his prized collection quickly disappear, piece by piece. Oh, he might yell at the others to stop, or he might even run around in a pathetic attempt to curtail their carnivorous behaviour. But it was always futile.

There were few happier moments in the life of a pre-teenager than “Scrambles!” Not only did it represent sheer joy and excitement...but every kid loves receiving free stuff by air mail.

Lunch Boxes

As with bubble gum cards, the first-ever lunch box based on a television show was for *Hopalong Cassidy* in 1950.

From that point on, lunch boxes would go on to immortalize literally hundreds of television shows and characters. Like bubble gum cards, the biggest-selling lunch boxes were usually those which depicted images from the most popular television shows. However, in addition to all of the standby favorites represented in cards, the list of lunch boxes was a much more padded one: *The A-Team, Adam-12, Alf, The Archies, The Banana Splits, Berenstain Bears, Bonanza, The Buccaneers, The Bugaloos, Bugs Bunny, Cabbage Patch Kids, Care Bears, Charlie Brown, Daniel Boone, Donnie and Marie, Dukes of Hazzard, Dudley Do-Right, Dick Tracy, Emergency, Even*

Knievel, The Fall Guy, Family Affair, Fat Albert, Flintstones, Fess Parker, Flipper, The Flying Nun, Fraggle Rock, Frontier Days, Garfield, G.I. Joe, Gene Autrey, Gentle Ben, Gomer Pyle, Goober and the Ghost Chasers, Grizzly Adams, The Harlem Globetrotters, Have Gun Will Travel, Hee Haw, He-Man and Masters of the Universe, Howdy Doody, Huckleberry Hound, The Jetsons, Josie and the Pussycats, Julia, Knight Rider, Land of the Lost, Lassie, Little House on the Prairie, The Muppet Show, Pac-Man, Popeye, Rocky and Bullwinkle, Sesame Street, Scooby Doo, Shari Lewis, Sigmund and the Sea Monsters, Smokey Bear, Snoopy, Soupy Sales, Speed Buggy, Spiderman, Smurfs, Super Friends, Transformers, Underdog, Wagon Train, The Waltons, Wild Bill Hickok, The Wild Wild West, Winnie the Pooh, Wonder Woman, Wrangler, Woody Woodpecker, Yogi Bear, and Zorro.

Since its inception in the 18th century, the lunch box was traditionally made of some sort of metal. In 1972, a group of Florida housewives complained that metal lunch boxes could be used as school-yard weapons which resulted in safety legislation eventually being passed. Since 1987, the majority of lunch boxes have been constructed with plastic or vinyl. School-yard weapons, ladies? Sheesh.

Left Overs

For every show that makes it as a hit, countless more fall short of the mark. Here is a list of some unlucky pilots that withered on the vine.

The Six Million Dollar Mandible

(Starring Lee Majors)

Astronaut Steve Austin slipped on a banana peel and landed face-first on a hard kitchen counter. The force of the fall knocked his lower jaw clean off. It was replaced with a shiny new bionic mandible; one that was better, stronger, *faster* -- and which enabled Steve to chew his food at super-human speeds. As busy as he was, finding the time to eat simply would never be a problem any more.

Needless to say, his chewing gum would always lose its flavor in a hurry. Steve was also fitted with a bionic eye, which enabled him to spot a potential meal from a mile away. He would constantly give The Bionic Woman the eye. And then she would give it right back again.

Her name was Jaime Sommers, and the two definitely had eyes for each other. Sommers would eventually leave Steve after he mistook her exposed kneecap for a mango and began to masticate it. She was sick and tired of Steve's embarrassing habit of masticating in public. Oh well, you know what they say: man come... man go.

Barney Miller Lite

(Starring Hal Linden, Steve Landesberg, and Abe Vigoda)

This knock-off was a 2nd-rate, watered-down version of *Barney Miller*. Where *Barney Miller* tasted great and satisfied on several different levels, *Barney Miller Lite* was just plain less filling. And talk about uninspired performances? While Abe Vigoba was playing "Fish"... the rest of the cast was playing "Go Fish".

Sandwich and Son

(Starring Redd Foxx and Demond Wilson)

Fred Sanford is notoriously lazy and rarely helps out around the junk yard. His exasperated son Lamont puts an ultimatum to his father: either start pulling your weight, or Lamont will pack up and move out. It wasn't the fact that Lamont was demanding, so much as he was *Demond*-ing. Terrified at the prospect of living alone, Fred goes to the Mayo Clinic and gets a hero sandwich surgically attached to his hand. This way, Fred would never be too far away from a snack. But, more importantly, it provided him with a great excuse to not do any work; for then the sandwich would get dirty. SPOILER ALERT: The sandwich spoiled.

Welcome Back, Ricotta
(Starring John Travolta and Gabe Kaplan)

Was considered a little too fresh for mainstream tastes. Audiences felt it belonged in the freezer. Not so much lactose-intolerant as it was *laughtose*-intolerant. Really left a terrible odor -- which took about four years to finally go away. Thank goodness somebody noticed the expiration date and finally tossed it.

The Young and the Breastless
(Starring Eric Braeden)

Nicky, Jill, Mrs. Chancellor, Lance, Paul, April, and Snapper, decide to throw a charity picnic for all of Genoa City's orphans. They planned to serve chicken breast. But when they go to pick up the order, they are told that someone has purchased all of the available chicken breasts. It was the town ogre, Victor Newman.

Victor had heard all about the plans for a picnic and did not approve of such frivolity and good will. The picnic ended up having to be canceled. All of the poor orphans cried. But Victor Newman had the time of his life.

He spent the day feet up, smoking Cuban cigars, drinking expensive wine, and overlooking the hundreds of unused boxes of raw chicken breasts that were slowly turning rancid in his cavernous, yet lonely basement.

Porterhouse on the Prairie
(Starring Michael Landon)

Charles Ingalls is a dirt-poor settler who has had it up to here with having to subsist on an all-vegetarian diet. He sizes up his assets: he has three strong, healthy daughters. He consults with his wife Caroline, and together they decide to sell Mary and Laura into slavery while keeping young Carrie. In return...the hungry trio receives a well-fattened beef cow on the hoof. In the days and weeks to come, Charles would be enjoying a bonanza on the ponderosa.

Salami Vice

(Starring Don Johnson and Philip Michael Thomas)

Eighties heartthrob, Johnson, runs through drug-infested Miami throwing his sausage around in expensive Italian suits. What a total hot dog this guy is. Audiences and critics agreed that "Crockett and Tubbs" were the best-dressed dicks in town.

Burger, She Wrote

(Starring Angela Lansbury and Tom Bosley)

Jessica Fletcher is a restaurant critic who moonlights as a nosy old hag. Every time she goes out to review a restaurant, somebody ends up dropping dead in front of her of apparent food poisoning. But was it really accidental food poisoning...or murder!

Whenever the cops arrest a suspect, only she and she alone knows that they have most likely apprehended the wrong person.

She then has to go about proving her case to save the poor slob from being barbecued, while bringing the real killer into the cops for a sound grilling. Otherwise...the guy is surely dead meat. Being a rather light eater, she doesn't require a pound of flesh: a quarter pounder hits the spot just fine.

It doesn't take much to keep herself together and in one piece. A freshly cracked egg in the morning usually does the trick. Yet without that egg she would literally fall to pieces.

Jessica doesn't use talcum powder after a shower. She prefers sprinkling herself with French Onion Soup mix to add extra flavor.

Married With Chili

(Starring Ed O'Neil, Katey Sagal,
Christina Applegate, and David Faustino)

The Bundys can never get a decent meal -- not with bon-bon popping Peggy in charge of the kitchen. Al, Kelly, and Bud come close to eating their beloved dog Buck on more than one occasion. Realizing that this has got to stop, Al encourages Peg to have an affair with a Mexican male stripper who is putting himself through cooking school. The Mexican works at a strip joint called "The South Pole" -- where Al, Kelly, and Bud often stop by to have a meal, drink a beer, and admire his skills with the hot, stiff pole that Peg has become so attached to.

Are You Smarter Than a Cheese Grater?
(Starring Jeff Foxworthy)

Many quiz and game shows attract some pretty stupid contestants -- especially those shows that feature a large spinning wheel, audience members wanting to "make a deal," or letters being turned over to spell out a common phrase. On *Are You Smarter Than A Cheese Grater*, host Jeff Foxworthy has his work cut out for him. It is his job to determine just how stupid a particular contestant is. He progressively works his way through such low-intelligence items as marbles, bowling balls, Q-Tips, fridge magnets, peach pits, and thimbles, before arriving at a cheese grater.

By this point, all of America is wrapped up in the tension, and they're all asking themselves the same question about the contestant at hand: "Are you smarter than a cheese grater?"

Dancing With the Sitars

(Hosted by Tom Bergeron)

This is India's version of *Dancing with the Stars.* After scoring big with an Indianized remake of the 80s film, *Urban Cowboy* (renamed, *Turban Cowboy*), Indian television executives decided it was a safe bet to plunder yet another dance-related property. Host Tom Bergeron pairs Indian celebrities *not* with a professional dance instructor...but with a sitar. The celebrity must then dance around with it to the hottest Hindustani hits.

The contestant who looks the least ridiculous wins. Top prize is -- you guessed it -- a stray street cow of their choice. You can tell that everybody's really embarrassed to be there...but they're just trying to curry favor.

"Come and get it!"

Thanks to the Food Network, food and cooking have never been bigger than they are right now. The Food Network began in 1993 in America, and the year 2000 in Canada. But the first cooking show on television was waaaay back in 1946 -- *I Love to Eat* was hosted by James Beard on NBC. The legendary Julia Child debuted on PBS in 1963.

In 2007, Joe Scarborough began hosting *Morning Joe* on MSNBC. But instead of ordinary carbohydrates, this particular blend of coffee contains plenty of "Scarborough-hydrates".

You don't have to look very far or wide to notice the powerful influence that cuisine has had on our society and culture. I mean, heck, even professional wrestling offered up "The Nacho Man" Randy Savage, Bruno Sammartuna, Hulk Hoagie, Griller Monsoon, Sweet Daddy Tzatziki, Chef Jay Strongbow, "Roti" Roddy Piper, and "Gassy" Freddie Blassie.

But back on Gilligan's Island...everybody suspected that the Skipper might have been having an affair with one of the girls. Either that or he was spending a lot of time preparing Chinese food. His fingers always smelled like Ginger.

Food for Peace in the Middle East

No sweat. Here's how to do it. Stop calling it The West Bank...start calling it The Food Bank.

Instead of G8 countries...V8 countries.

Instead of the United Nations...the United Rations.

Instead of a Prime Minister...a Prime Ribister.

Instead of the Gaza Strip...the Mi Casa es su Casa Strip.

Instead of the Star Spangled Banner...the Star Spangled Banana.

Instead of Moammar Gadhafi...Mallomars and Taffy

The only thing necessary to join the union would be access to a delicious Ham radio. That's because when it comes to food and beverages...we're all pretty much on the same wavelength. Crisis solved. What was so hard about that?

And another thing...if people from Palestine can refer to themselves as Palestinians, why shouldn't people from Italy be able to refer to themselves as Pasta-inians? Moreover, if people from Slovakia can refer to themselves as Slovakians, why shouldn't people from Greece be allowed to refer to themselves as Souvlakians? A little borrowing never hurt anybody. It is akin to asking your neighbor if you may simply borrow a cup of milk or sugar to help with a favorite recipe.

Indeed, a country's name is often reflective of the people who live there. After all, you wouldn't want to live in a country named "Cramps," would you? Or a city named "Dumpster"? So why not name your country after a favorite food?

For example, a typical person interested in traveling to an exciting vacation destination might ponder thusly: "You know, next year I think I'm going to spend a nice, relaxing summer in Jerk Chicken. Or, maybe do some skiing in Northern Salami Sandwich. And, what could be more romantic than Kung Pao Chicken in the spring?"

The possibilities are truly mouth-watering. As long as you have the stomach for it.

People are basically identical the world over. We are all interested in the same things. We simply want a decent life where we can work, fall in love, raise some kids, masturbate in private...and hopefully have some curtains nearby to wipe off on.

I grew up in a predominantly Jewish neighborhood, where all of us kids breathed the same air, played the same games, and spoke the same language: the language of FUN! At home, our respective families would settle down at night and enjoy some of the most popular TV shows of the era. The viewing habits of my Jewish friends' families were practically identical to those of my own family.

We watched *Mannix*...they watched *Manischewitz.* We watched *Gentle Ben*...they watched *Yentl Ben.* We watched *All in the Family*...they watched *Saul in the Family.*

Ditto with popular music. We listened to "I Should Have Known Better"...they listened to "Meshugenah Better". We listened to "Hunk-a, Hunk-a Burning Love"... they listened to "Hanukkah, Hanukkah Burning Love". We listened to "Stuck in the Middle With You"...they listened to "Schmuck in the Middle With You".

It was the same with movies. We watched *Close Encounters of the Third Kind*...they watched *Kosher Encounters of the Third Kind.* We watched *Home Alone*... they watched *Shalom Alone.* We watched *Hannah and Her Sisters*... they watched *Rosh Hashanah and Her Sisters.*

We also suffered from similar physical ailments. We got leprosy...they got schleprosy. We got sores accompanied by pus...they got tsuris accompanied by putz. We got poison ivy...they got poison oy vey.

We fed our dog Kibbles 'n Bits...they fed theirs Kibbutz 'n Kibitz. Our dog had a muzzle we would kiss... theirs had a mazel tov and bupkiss. Our dog would never attack its masters...theirs would never attack its matzahs. (Speaking of dogs, scientists recently announced that they now have DNA testing for dogs so that their owners can know for sure what breed the dog is. Hopefully, this will also help free thousands of innocent dogs out there who were wrongly imprisoned for crimes they didn't commit. Sure, there are some hardened killers out there, but not every dog is Jack the Ripper...or Yom the Kippur.)

Oh, and circumcision? Well, no male wants to think about having a piece of his penis lopped off. I'm guessing this is the main reason why they do it to the guy when he's still just a baby -- so he won't have any memory of the horrific and excruciating event. That's why, if there's one thing we do agree on, it's that "Ignorance is bris". (Rumpelstiltskin is a Grimm Fairy Tale. Rumpleforeskin is just plain grim.)

I suppose the most glaring difference between my Jewish friends and I was when it came down to doing writing assignments in class. They were always looking up words. I was always looking up dresses.

If someone was an outright fool (or "golem"), I wouldn't hesitate to say it directly to their face. That's because I've always been one to golem as I see 'em; whether they come from Golem A or Golem B.

But I did have the honor of being the Best Man at a Jewish wedding. Sure, stepping on the glass until it breaks was fun, but my favorite part was when all the guys in the wedding party converged to hoist the groom up into the air and parade him around for a while. I felt like I'd won the Stanley Cup.

Food That Resembles Genitalia

Watching people eat certain foods in public can be very educational. And hilarious. It's an exercise in psychology, almost. No woman involved in the process of slowly plunging a banana into her gaping mouth can be so oblivious as to not be aware of the blatant, racy imagery she is conjuring up for the world to see. And you don't have to be a pervert to see it. But it helps.

In an effort to avoid this embarrassing and uncomfortable pre-dick-amint, a more cautious, experienced woman would sooner break off little pieces of the banana at a time, instead, and then very stealthily insert the now un-penis-like-looking morsels into her mouth. Still others would rather leave it in their lunch bag entirely.

Many are simply not able to resist the urge at all... and will just break out laughing. Some will conjure up a suggestive Mona Lisa smile. Others will get all self-conscious and may even turn beet red. Then, if you ask them why they're laughing, they'll try to deflect it by responding with something nonchalant like: "Oh, I just thought of something funny that happened the other day, that's all".

But the truth is something much simpler: they probably just witnessed the usually-demure and somewhat prudish secretary in the next cubicle over going down on a Tootsie Pop like a world-class porn star. Who among us wouldn't be amused at such a spectacle?

But any way you slice it, there's no getting around the fact that many of the foods we eat on a regular basis can appear rather...*provocative.*

Men

Penis:

Banana ("Say yellow to my little friend!")

Plantain (Favorite of ladies everywhere. Looks like a banana; but it's much, much, harder.)

Zucchini ("Most people think he's a vegetable; but he's actually a fruit.")

Cucumber (If he was any grosser…he'd be grocer.)

Pickle (Vlasic the Impaler? That guy was a real Dill-do)

Gherkin (It rhymes with "jerkin'".)

Chili Pepper (Self-pollinating; hot, hot, hot sauce.)

Parsnip (Most men are uncomfortable around any food with the word "snip" in it.)

Popsicle (Slides perfectly into any woman's "ice box".)

Lollipop (For ladies who prefer a disproportionately big knob.)

Sausage (They don't call them "bangers" for nothing.)

Celery (Everybody's going green these days.)

Breadsticks (Perfect for whore d'oeuvres.)

Carrot (It's true that the penis has only one eye. But this one has excellent vision.)

Cannoli (Comes complete with ricotta and/or custard filling.)

Hot Dog (You'd never swallow another one if you knew where it's been.)

Ice Cream Cones (The x-rated technique necessary to eat them deserves an award. Or, at the very least…a Polaroid.)

Testicles:

Chicken Balls (A man this well endowed is usually dim some. Speaking of dim bulbs, George W. Bush actually thinks an electrician is someone who fixes elections.)

Wontons (He'll make you drop to your Cantonese and beg for more.)

Grape Cluster (Pick them off and watch them swing!)

Plums (Men seek them out in jams; women seek them out in jammies.)

Prunes (Rip Van Wrinkle?)

Dried Figs (They are filled with seeds...and hang in twos when they grow.)

Onions (Also known as "Bulbs"; are attached to a single, firm, vertical shoot; have been known to make women teary-eyed.)

Whole Walnuts (Speaking of trees...In 1998, Sonny Bono slammed into a tree while skiing, and died. He was a very "poplar" singer. Witnesses said he looked like he was caught in the headlights. I guess that's why Cher called him "dear" for all those years. Although Sonny's stock in the entertainment world continued to plummet, Cher's would continue to rise. Sonny was happy for Cher's success and would benefit greatly from his association with her. After all, he used to be a major Cher holder. Towards the end, he didn't have many hits, but that last hit left quite an impression -- on the tree. In these touchy times of Meat Eating vs. Vegetarianism, people often wonder if Sonny was carnivorous. Well, all I can tell you is that he ended up rather "coniferous". Like most people, he enjoyed a good lager now and then. In fact, it was a team of loggers, familiar with the hollow thud of bone upon pine, who originally dialed 911. When the owner of the resort asked his wife what the hell Sonny Bono was doing there, she replied: "I told him he could crash at our place.")

Women

Vagina:

Cheeseburger (Have it HER way.)

Oysters ("We shucked for hours; then I left her a nice pearl necklace.")

Mussels (We put the "broth" back in brothel.)

Clams (Beware of giant clams: one almost devoured Robin whole in TV's Batman.)

Snails (Hygiene is of the utmost important. Otherwise, they can leave tracks like slugs.)

Watermelon Slice (Seedless, preferably.)

Strawberries (Always a welcome treat after spending a long, hot day in the bush.)

Taco (Will fall out all over the place unless you handle it properly. Be sure to keep plenty of napkins handy.)

Lasagna (Multi-layered feast. But is that meat I see in there...or is it all cheese?)

Shelled Walnuts (I can pop them in my mouth all day; but hopefully she's not a nut cracker.)

Stingrays/Manta Rays (There are plenty of other fish in the sea.)

Fortune Cookie ("Um, Honey...this small piece of paper with a message typed on it just fell out of there."

Honorary "non-food" mentions:
- Somebody lying on their side while sticking their tongue out.
- Medulla Oblongata (Anterior View) *(Now that's what I call brain food!)*
- Those oval-shaped, rubber squeeze change purses.
- A conch sea shell.
- Ace of Spades *(This queen is always flush for some good stud action.)*

Breasts:

Squash (Are of the "gourd" family. Nice tits will drive most guys out of their gourd.)

Eggplants (Needs lots of sunlight. Very sensitive to WASPS. Plans to retire to Belly Acres, Florida.)

Coconuts (Grown on Palm trees. Men like to palm women's coconuts.)

Anything with a cherry on top (Like "Half-Baked Alaska" -- Sarah Palin's favorite dessert.)

Haggis (You savor everything about her: her heart... her liver...her stomach...her lungs...)

Fried Eggs ("Come on over, baby, Whole Lot of Bacon Goin' On!")

Jell-O (They shimmer. They shake. But I don't like Bill Cosby's face drooling all over them.)

Pears (Bad things comes in threes; good things come in pears.)

The 12 Foods of Christmas

No man is an island. Well, except for Cuba Gooding Jr. Cuba is an island.

Holidays, in general, have traditionally occupied a special place in the hearts of family, friends...and shameless moochers who like to show up to get their filthy mitts on free food and drinks. But what with people working so much these days, and sometimes even living in different cities, Christmas often represents the *only* occasion throughout the entire year when we are able to spend quality time around the people we grew up with. Thank God. Fucking idiots.

The important thing is to keep active so that the time doesn't drag. I quickly exchange greetings with my Bother-in-law. Then with my Stripper-in-law.

And, before I can say "what did I do to deserve this?" it's already time for a light food-teaser. Followed by an aperitif. Or seven. With the main corpse still broiling away for another hour or so, there's plenty of time yet to get into the festive holiday mood.

Now, don't forget to keep basting that bird! Because, remember: what's good for the grease is good for the gander. Speaking of Christmas Goose, I was born in September -- which is the ninth month of the year. That makes me a Virgo.

Now, I don't know about you, but I don't believe in any of that astrology/horoscope mumbo-jumbo. I am interested in astronomy, however...mainly because it sounds like "pastrami".

Do you know what it means if you were born in September? It means your parents had sex on either Christmas or New Year's.

And being that I'm the last-born child in our family, and my parents were Roman Catholic...that was very likely the last goose my mother would ever receive.

Are board games your idea of a delightful time-passer? Me too! There is nothing I enjoy more than playing a few friendly rounds of Trivial Prosciutto.

As we slowly (but surely) approach the point of being looped -- playing on a loop in the background are the loopy sounds of Christmas carols, sung by the likes of Luciano Panzarotti, Paprika Caruso, Salmon Davis Jr., Sardine Martin, Mortadella Fitzgerald, Fleetwood Mac & Cheese, Manwich Steamroller, the New Figs on the Block, Fruity Garland, and the country stylings of Ribeye McEntire.

But to *really* stimulate our appetites, we first pass around some of the finest Herb: Herb Alpert and the Marijuana Brass.

I've always felt that the lamest Christmas carol of all time was probably, "All I Want For Christmas Is My Two Front Teeth" -- which debuted in 1948. On the positive side, the song does act as a reminder to practice effective dental hygiene. For, after indulging in a rich and fattening Christmas feast, it's important that you clean the tooth, the whole tooth, and nothing but the tooth.

"Kiss my foot -- I've got mistle-toe!"

Uh-oh... (shudder)...that must be none other than dear old Uncle Hackney I hear at the door. Wait...yup, it's him. He's been saying, "Kiss my foot -- I've got mistle-toe!" for going on 40 years now. Usually about every twenty minutes, or so. Not unlike the traffic and weather update on your least-favorite radio station.

Uncle Hack lived in an old age home, and Christmas was one of the few times all year when he was allowed out. Whenever it was Karaoke night at the home, he and three other fun-loving seniors with stars in their eyes (glaucoma) would dress up as a cowboy, an Indian, a construction worker, and a cop, and go on to give a rousing rendition of the 70's hit song, "Y.M.C.A.". Since the seniors all suffered from incontinence, and wore adult diapers, the staff soon took to referring to them as "The Spillage People". My sediments exactly.

Unc's questionable hygiene practices, combined with his legendary love of Clint Eastwood movies, led us all to affectionately refer to him as "Dirty, Hairy". ("I know what you're thinking, punk. Did I shower six days ago, or only five?")

"Kiss my foot – I've got mistle-toe!" Yes, ha-ha...that was a good one, Unc!

My favorite Christmas carol has forever been "The Twelve Foods of Christmas". It's somewhat similar to "The Twelve Days of Christmas"...only this version sticks to your ribs better.

On the first day of Christmas
My true love sent to me
A bar fridge in a pantry.

On the second day of Christmas
My true love sent to me
Two fertile eggs,
And a bar fridge in a pantry.

On the third day of Christmas
My true love sent to me
Three fresh fruits,
Two fertile eggs,
And a bar fridge in a pantry.

On the fourth day of Christmas
My true love sent to me
Four thawing steaks,
Three fresh fruits,
Two fertile eggs,
And a bar fridge in a pantry.

On the fifth day of Christmas
My true love sent to me
FIVE COLA DRINKS!
Four thawing steaks,
Three fresh fruits,
Two fertile eggs,
And a bar fridge in a pantry.

On the sixth day of Christmas
My true love sent to me
Six geeks filleting,
FIVE COLA DRINKS!
Four thawing steaks,
Three fresh fruits,
Two fertile eggs,
And a bar fridge in a pantry.

On the seventh day of Christmas
My true love sent to me
Seven Swanson Dinners,
Six geeks filleting,
FIVE COLA DRINKS!
Four thawing steaks,
Three fresh fruits,
Two fertile eggs,
And a bar fridge in a pantry.

On the eighth day of Christmas
My true love sent to me
Eight pounds of Milk Duds,
Seven Swanson Dinners,
Six geeks filleting,
FIVE COLA DRINKS!
Four thawing steaks,
Three fresh fruits,
Two fertile eggs,
And a bar fridge in a pantry.

On the ninth day of Christmas
My true love sent to me
Nine fancy lettuce,
Eight pounds of Milk Duds,
Seven Swanson Dinners,
Six geeks filleting,
FIVE COLA DRINKS!
Four thawing steaks,
Three fresh fruits,
Two fertile eggs,
And a bar fridge in a pantry.

On the tenth day of Christmas
My true love sent to me
Ten Pop Tarts leaping,
Nine fancy lettuce,
Eight pounds of Milk Duds,
Seven Swanson Dinners,
Six geeks filleting,
FIVE COLA DRINKS!
Four thawing steaks,
Three fresh fruits,
Two fertile eggs,
And a bar fridge in a pantry.

On the eleventh day of Christmas
My true love sent to me
Eleven pickled peppers,

Ten Pop Tarts leaping,
Nine fancy lettuce,
Eight pounds of Milk Duds,
Seven Swanson Dinners,
Six geeks filleting,
FIVE COLA DRINKS!
Four thawing steaks,
Three fresh fruits,
Two fertile eggs,
And a bar fridge in a pantry.

On the twelfth day of Christmas
My true love sent to me
Twelve turkey drumsticks,
Eleven pickled peppers,
Ten Pop Tarts leaping,
Nine fancy lettuce,
Eight pounds of Milk Duds,
Seven Swanson Dinners,
Six geeks filleting,
FIVE COLA DRINKS!
Four thawing steaks,
Three fresh fruits,
Two fertile eggs,
And a bar fridge in a pantry.

See? Pure holiday magic.

"Come and get it!"

Ah!...at long last we hear the old battle cry from the old battle axe (Mom) which we've all been waiting for. (Remember: the sooner you eat, the sooner you can get the hell out of there.) Next comes the most dangerous part; the part where everyone scurries around in a desperate attempt to get the best seat at the table. It sort of resembles a game of "Musical Chairs": the type that might be played by rival psychotic killers.

Finally, we occupy our places just as the main corpse is being sliced up and served. (I said "occupy," not "octopi" -- but you wouldn't know it judging by the dozens of jumbled and arms and legs, all intertwined and slithering about like greedy tentacles belonging to a squadron of malevolent sea creatures desperately intent on being the first to secure a delicious prey item.)

In our family, the distinct honor of carving the main corpse has almost always been bestowed upon the volunteer who displayed the most enthusiasm for the task; the candidate whose entire sense of self-worth seemed to depend entirely on their being "in charge" during pivotal moments such as this (see: the male relative with the smallest penis).

Mmmm...smells fantastic! That's how you know when something is really good "human food": you look up. No vultures flying overhead? That means there's a low bacteria count...which means dig in.

"Save room for dessert!"

Speaking of human food...myself, I've never been much of a dessert man -- unlike Jeffrey Dahmer. Dahmer loved to treat himself to a big hunk of Human Meringue Pie, topped with a couple of scoops of Ben and Jerry's. Not the ice cream -- just some guy he picked up named Ben and another named Jerry.

It is very common for people to confuse the spellings of "dessert" and "desert" with one another. But there is an easy way to remember the differences. Allow me to help.

. A dessert is something which makes you fat. Except instead of a double chin...it sports a double "s".

. A desert is a very hot place. It's *so* hot that it caused that extra "s" to sweat right off of your dessert.

So take heart. The next time somebody calls you a "fat ass"...they may actually be calling you a fat 's'. Not as bad.

Now if somebody calls you a "fat ass piece of shit"... that's different. It means you probably do have a fat ass. The "piece of shit" part simply functions as a confirmation.

A Republican Christmas

Sarah Palin likes to blast animals from a helicopter. She shoots Moose, Bears, Reindeer, and Elk (an Elk-aholic?). Sarah inadvertently dispatched of Dasher, Donner, and Blitzen using a high-powered rifle, causing Santa endless heartache. (Coincidentally, Santa can see Alaska from the North Pole!) She then campaigned to have "Dancer" replaced by "Bristol," using the logic that Bristol is now a dancer too.

But what's really interesting is how Sarah completely avoids any mention of Comet.

(That's because the very existence of comets suggests that the universe is older than 5,000 years old... and that the theory of evolution is correct.)

Sarah's good friend and political ally -- former rocker, Ted Nugent -- often accompanies her out on the hunt. In reality, Sarah likes to have Ted around -- not so much because they share an unsettling urge to kill things -- but because compared to this guy, she looks perfectly sane, well-balanced, and stable. Not very many people in the world could have pulled that one off. But Ted has.

Ted can be seen on Youtube giving the following rant during one of his recent concerts.

"I was in Chicago last week, I was in Chicago, I said, 'Hey Obama, you might want to suck on one of these, you punk!' (holds up a machine gun in each hand). You know, Obama, he's a piece of shit and I told him to suck on my machine gun, let's hear it for him. And then I was in New York, I said, I said, 'Hey Hilary, you might want to ride one of these into the sunset, you worthless bitch!' (holds up a machine gun in his right hand). How about Barbara Boxer, she might want to suck on my machine gun (holds up a machine gun in each hand). Hey Diane Feinstein, ride on one of these, you worthless whore (holds up a machine gun in each hand). Hey Christians...FREEDOM!!!! (holds up a machine gun in each hand)." No problems here.

Back to hunting... Nobody could ever accuse Ted Nugent of not looking out for the welfare of wild animals. He looks out for them, alright...through a precision scope. Nor could anybody ever accuse Ted of not doing what's best for endangered species.

On this one particular occasion, Ted noticed that an animal appeared to be quite rare. So he left it on the rotisserie for about another half an hour.

Food Cliches

Example:

"You have to break a few eggs to make an omelet"

What did the fertility specialist say to the fat woman who kept showing up at his office every morning? "Look lady, I told you a thousand times: I fix eggs and ovaries -- not eggs over easy!"

Speaking of gynecology -- opportunities for steady, good-paying careers are incredibly tough to find these days. But I hear there are a lot of openings in that area.

Since the beginning of recorded time, people have been using food analogies when trying to illustrate a point. It's universal. You will find this to be true anywhere in the world where people eat food. However, this is not true in the places where people do not eat food. That's because they don't eat food... which means they're dead.

"The apple doesn't fall far from the tree"

It's amazing how people want to make this sound like a bad thing. What do you want to do -- set up a trampoline under the tree so they bounce farther? You don't see tomatoes falling very far from the vine, either, do you? Or carrots pole-vaulting out of the ground? They're apples, for Pete's sake -- not Indian rubber balls.

"An apple a day keeps the doctor away"

Speaking of doctors, an "Oncologist" is a cancer specialist. It's not a doctor who is always "on call". In fact, an apple a day will not keep the doctor away at all. That's simply an advertising slogan put out by apple growers in the early 1900s in an effort to increase sales.

"You're comparing apples and oranges"

Most European countries use "apples and pears" instead of oranges. But either way... you really need to get out of that supermarket and get a life.

"Don't upset the apple cart"

How the hell does one upset an apple cart, exactly? Do you borrow money from it and then avoid its phone calls?

"How do you like them apples?"

This phrase is said to have originated in World War 1 by Allied soldiers who would throw small bombs at the enemy which resembled toffee apples. When I was a kid going out on Halloween, we would occasionally receive apples with razor blades stuck in them. I suppose soldiers would have thrown these apples at enemies who appeared to need a shave?

"Bringing home the bacon"

This term originated in 12th century England. So the legend goes, any man who could prove that he had not argued with his wife for a year and a day would be awarded a side of bacon. Unfortunately, the deal did not apply to men who already had a fat pig waiting for them at home.

"It saved my bacon"

Isn't that what a Piggy Bank is for? That's just some more worthless tripe on my part.

"He's going bananas"

Strange, I've heard of men going bald before... but never of men who lose their hair, and then start to grow bananas instead.

"Somebody spilled the beans"

This is an American idiom from the early 20th century. It means to talk out of turn, to reveal a secret, or confess to something. But it probably got its start when some klutz actually went and knocked over a bunch of beans. In World War II, the term "Loose Lips Might Sink Ships" was meant to guard against people possibly giving useful information to enemy spies. And, of course, in this particular case…they'd be spilling Navy beans.

"It's not worth a hill of beans"

Especially if they're has-beans.

"That's my bread and butter over there"

Some people are so attached to their food, they just aren't happy unless they can introduce it around to people.

"He knows which side his bread is buttered on"

He didn't always used to know, mind you. But then he got sick of getting butter all over his hand. That's when he really started paying attention.

"It's the greatest thing since sliced bread"

Sliced bread was first sold in Missouri in 1928 by the Chillicothe Baking Company. In 1930, Wonder bread began marketing it nationwide. The original slogan by Chillicothe was, "The greatest forward step in the baking industry since bread was wrapped." But that didn't quite make the cut. It's no Wonder.

"Grab the bull by the horns"

I'll take the experts' word for it on this one. I have limited experience with bulls. But this much I do know: grabbing them by the testicles tends to make them rather hornery. I mean ornery. So, yes…stick to the horns.

"She has another bun in the oven"

Somebody ought to tell the tramp to keep her oven door closed a little more often. This kid will be her thirteenth -- a perfect Baker's Dozen.

"Butter somebody up"

To butter somebody up would be to cover them with praise and flattery as you would a slice of bread with butter. Of course, the phrase may have an entirely different connotation in Japan, where overworked transit employees are constantly having to squeeze that last obese passenger on to an already-crowded subway car.

"Too many cooks spoil the broth"

Good lord -- have you guys ever heard of mouth-wash? Your broth smells terrible!

"It was a piece of cake"

Possibly first coined in a 1936 poem by Ogden Nash, " The Primrose Path": "Her picture's in the papers now, and life's a piece of cake". But that reference was more indicative of the cake representing something "sweet," "special," or "rewarding" -- and not so much the "simple," "easy," or "it's a snap" we've come to associate it with.

"Nutty as a fruitcake"

This term was coined in 1935 by two competing bakeries in the American South who both had access to lots and lots of cheap nuts...and I don't mean rednecks. "Nutty" (meaning "insane") was first used in 1821.

"That's just icing on the cake"

Two questions: 1. Why are they playing hockey on a cake. 2. Why the hell did that idiot ref call icing?

"You can't have your cake and eat it to"

But if you're a fan of All in the Family...you can have your Archie, and Edith too.

"It's like taking candy from a baby"

In the 1800s this term originally referred to a task that was difficult or even impossible. It eventually came to mean the exact opposite. I believe the original version to be the more accurate one. Just imagine trying to pry some gooey, sticky candy from a baby's tightly-closed little fist, or right out of his slobbering, drooling mouth -- and the whole time the kid is bawling his eyes out while people are giving you dirty looks. See? Not so easy.

"Leading someone along with a carrot on a stick"

To lead someone along with carrot on a stick means you're getting them to perform a task by baiting them with what appears to be a reward of a meal. Of course, they're never intended to actually reach the reward. They're meant to keep slaving away all day while chasing that damn carrot. You really are a heartless piece of shit, you know that?

"Who cut the cheese?"

In Britain in the early 1800s the term "cheeser" was used to describe a flatulence event. By the late 1800s the term "cut" was now used to describe the act of expelling gas. By 1899 the act of breaking wind was described as "to cut your finger". The expression "cut the cheese" made its formal debut in the mid 1960s -- likely because it smelled eerily similar to when you slice into some particularly raunchy European cheeses for the first time.

Oh, and for your information..."The First Cut Is The Deepest" is not a song about cheese farts.

"Life is a bowl of cherries"

Comes from the 1931 hit song by Rudy Vallee, "Life is Just a Bowl of Cherries": "Life is just a bowl of cherries, Don't take it serious, It's too mysterious, You work, You save, You worry so, But you can't take your dough, When you go, go, go."

"She lost her cherry"/"She had her cherry popped"

These two are intimately connected. For the full rundown on their meaning, just ask any guy named "Hymen".

"Don't count your chickens before they're hatched"

From the Aesop fable, "The Milkmaid and Her Pail," written in the 1st century B.C.C. (Before Counting Chickens).

"Clam up"

To "clam up" means to keep your mouth shut, remain silent on some particular matter, or refuse or withhold information. Any member of the Mob who was not skilled at clamming up would inevitably find himself sleeping with the fishes.

"Happy as a clam"

Borrowed from the phrase, "Happy as a clam at high water" -- for this is when clams are at their safest from marauding low-tide predators. Hey, I know how irritable I can get when a marauding predator is looking to crack me open and eat me.

"Wake up and smell the coffee"

This was first used by either Dear Abby or Ann Landers -- nobody can remember for sure. I'm guessing none of their readers were tea drinkers.

"Dollars to donuts"

This is a rhetorical wager you'd make if you felt absolutely, positively certain about an expected outcome; so much so that you'd be willing to put up some of your hard-earned cash money against someone else's worthless donuts. Um, first of all, let's get one thing straight: there is no such thing as a worthless donut.

"That's the way the cookie crumbles"

From the1920s. Its modern counterpart is the somewhat blunter, "shit happens". Or, for those who prefer crackers: "Life's a Ritz, then you die".

"Smart cookie"/"Tough cookie"

Originating in the 1940s, the term "cookie" was generally applied to women or children...or anyone with chocolate chips, fudge, or raisins in their stool.

"Caught with his hand in the cookie jar"

This simply means that someone was caught in the act of doing something they shouldn't have. Of course, it may also mean that the poor guy was inadvertently snagged by a super-voracious, man-eating cookie.

"Wait till the cows come home"

This phrase came to be in the 16th century. It refers to something which isn't expected to happen any time soon. That's because cows are notorious for taking their sweet, cud-muching time, and are notorious for being completely unconcerned with the time. Plus, it sounds a heck of a lot less offensive than "Wait till the Jamaicans come home".

"Cool as a cucumber"

Dates back to the 1500s as a way of describing somebody who was calm under pressure. Scientists would eventually discover that cucumbers are some 20 degrees cooler inside than outside...sort of like the first air-conditioned vegetable.

"Raking in the dough"/"Rolling in the dough"

Methinks that perhaps, just maybe, you might have used too much dough for that homemade bread recipe you clipped out of the newspaper. I mean, I can understand you needing a rolling pin...but a rake?

"If it looks like a duck, and it walks like a duck, and it quacks like a duck..."

Then you can be pretty sure that some bloodthirsty, kill-happy hunters are hiding in the weeds waiting to blow its cute little head off.

"Slippery as an eel"

As a scuba-diving Dean Martin once sang: "When a fish bites your thigh, and the pain makes you cry, that's a Moray!"

"Don't put all your eggs in one basket"

This is an ancient phrase suggesting that you should spread out your assets, or diversify. That way, if a tragedy hits, you won't be left with nothing. Then, we have the updated version offered up by Mark Twain in Pudd'nhead Wilson: "Put all your eggs in one basket -- and watch that basket!" Sheesh...must have been a lot of paranoid egg shoppers in Twain's time.

"Fishing for compliments"

Sounds like a great idea for a reality show featuring spoiled-brat Hollywood celebrities. Except that they should use real baited hooks.

"I've got bigger fish to fry"

There's nothing more annoying than an impertinent short order cook who talks back when you place an order.

"It's a fine kettle of fish"

Word of advice: kettles made of metal are much, much more durable.

"She drinks like a fish"

But, man, just look at those fins on her!

"He sleeps with the fishes"

This is classic dialogue from The Godfather, recited by Corleone family soldier, Sal Tessio (Abe Vigoda), regarding his much-feared but recently-murdered brother-in-arms, Luca Brasi. It means that someone is dead, and likely lying at the bottom of the ocean. On a related matter, fish don't really sleep in the normal sense. They haven't got eyelids. They enter a rest state...and I don't mean Florida.

"Your goose is cooked"

This phrase is derived from a 15th century Czechoslovakian Catholic reformer named John Hus. In Czhekoslovakian, "Hus" means "goose". In 1415, he attended a papal council which convicted him of (surprise!) heresy. He was sentenced to burn at the stake.

This was a favorite tactic of that all-loving, forgiving, understanding, benevolent, and completely-secure-within-itself Catholic Church. But to Hus's loyal supporters...they saw their beloved "goose" literally being cooked before their eyes.

"I heard it through the grapevine"

Soon after the telegraph was first implemented in 1844, the term "grapevine telegraph" was coined. It referred to the manner in which news was now beginning to spread by word of mouth, as if attached to a network of vines. The song, "I Heard it through the Grapevine" became a hit for numerous artists, including Smokey

Robinson and the Miracles, Gladys Knight and the Pips, and Creedence Clearwater Revival. But perhaps the most definitive version belongs to Marvin Gaye -- whose rendition remains the Motown song with the most weeks ever at #1, with seven.

Gaye would die a few short years later, when the incensed father he had been feuding with" telegraphed" a bullet through his son's heart. Ms. Knight has since put on about 350 lbs. Her new group will be called "Gladys Knight and the Chip Dips".

"Red herring"

This term originated in 19th century Britain. As a result of the smoking process used to preserve them, herrings would become red and pungent. These fish would then be smeared across the terrain to throw any blood-hounds off of someone's track. The herrings finally quit smoking once they learned it leads to cancer and emphysema.

"You can catch more flies with honey than with vinegar"

Valuable information...if I'm ever hard up for flies.

"Selling like hotcakes"

Comes from mid-19th century America, where hotcakes always sold effortlessly at church socials, picnics, fairs, etc. Hotcakes are more commonly called "pancakes" and were invented in Britain. Women who wear "pancake" are very often quite hot. Some even come from Britain! But remember, ladies... too much "griddle" leads to "girdle".

"When life gives you lemons...make lemonade"

When hooker gives you crabs...make crab cakes.

"He couldn't cut the mustard"

To "cut" mustard meant you would add vinegar to it to lessen the bitter taste and improve its flavor. Someone who could cut the mustard was considered a highly skilled individual. As far as we know, it was never anybody's job to "cut the ketchup," or "cut the relish". And I don't even want to consider what "cut the crap" entails.

"He's sowing his wild oats"

A "wild oat" is actually a stubborn weed which invades many farmers' fields throughout Europe. The only way to control them is to manually walk through the crops and remove them one-by-one. For farmers, this is considered an extremely wasteful use of one's precious time. Alright, but how then did the phrase receive its sexual connotation?

Well, personally, I've never considered women "weeds". However, that wouldn't preclude me from spraying one in the face with DDT, or turning a flame thrower on her, if she couldn't take a hint and get lost when I tell her that it's over.

"The world is my oyster"

From Shakespeare's, "The Merry Wives of Windsor". Shakespeare loved coming up with food references. As a matter of fact, he came up with more food references than you could Shake a Speare at. Or, a sword, if you want to be a sore-head about it. And you know what they say: live by the sore-head, die by the sore-head.

"Flat as a pancake"

But I'm sure she has a nice personality!

"She has a peaches and cream complexion"

OK, so let me get this straight. Her face is off-orange colored, un-skimmed, triple-layered, with large pits? I think I'd prefer a "Peaches & Herb" complexion. That way, her face would look more...reunited.

"Easy as pie"

First, to be fair, you must cut the pie evenly. And as any mathematician will tell you... Pie = 3.14159265 slices.

"It's a political hot potato"

I agree that hot potatoes can harm a politician. Many have emerged severely damaged or even scarred. That's why I believe that politicians should be forced to wear oven mitts.

"Everything's coming up roses"

I knew I shouldn't have eaten all those roses. Although no longer such a widespread practice, the fact is that rose petals are quite edible and have been consumed since ancient times.

"Rub salt in the wound"

Salt has traditionally been applied to wounds to help prevent infection. Unfortunately, its inherent stinging also contributed further pain and suffering. To "rub salt in a wound" was originally considered a good thing. It meant you were potentially helping to save someone's life.

But now, people are just too chicken, and will go to great lengths to avoid salt. I'm with them. Everybody knows paprika makes the better dry rub.

"He's a wolf in sheep's clothing"

Sounds like somebody is in serious need of a body waxing.

"She's a snake in the grass"

My Mamba always warned me about girls like you.

"A spoonful of sugar helps the medicine go down"

Ovaltine has lots of sugar. A Teen with an Ovula is an Ovular Teen. Many Ovular Offices have interns who drink Ovaltine. A spoonful of Ovaltine helps the intern go down.

"The way to a man's heart is through his stomach"

Not entirely factual. I once dated a forensic pathologist. She insisted that the way to a man's heart was through his rib cage. She even showed me the saw she uses. Twice. Each time directly after an argument.

"Eat, drink, and be merry"

Unless, of course, you're former FBI chief, and famous cross-dresser, J. Edgar Hoover. As everyone now knows, Hoover preferred to eat, drink, and be "Mary".

"There's no such thing as a free lunch"

Yes there is. You just need to have some really stupid friends and co-workers in your life.

Fast Food: Legitimate Beef?

Ever look at a McDonald's cheeseburger? It looks like an S.O.S pad with a melted credit card on top. Many fast food joints like to advertise how their burgers are made of 100% pure beef, or beef by-products. But are they really 100% pure beef...or is that mostly bull? And what the hell part of a cow does a "by-product" come from? Past research has indicated that the beef content in many fast food outlets is probably much closer to between 30% - 60%; the rest being comprised of cereal or filler.

Now of the 30% - 60% that's actually meat, yes -- 100% of *that* would be pure beef. But here's the thing. Technically, *anything* that comes off of a cow is 100% pure beef! Well, except for a rodeo rider being thrown off its back.

Unfortunately, that includes the eyes, the brain, the ears, the snout, the stomach, the tail, the bones, the lungs, the spleen, the intestines, the fat, the scraps, the kidneys, the blood, the gristle, the vagina, and, yes...the asshole.

Again, I'm not referring to the cowboy who's being thrown off. He may or may not be an asshole. I don't even know the guy. Ah, what the hell -- he walks around in a dumb cowboy hat and boots all the time, right? I think it's safe to say that he probably is an asshole.

Next, you stuff all of those yummy ingredients into a grinder, fine-mince them all into an unrecognizable paste, add a tractor-load load of artificial flavoring and coloring, and....voila!

Fast food establishments are notoriously difficult to pin down when it comes to having to divulge exactly what it is that they put in their food. It's tough to find a Colonel of truth in anything they say. On top of that, there is no shortage of self-serving propaganda being spread by their advocacy groups, who are well-armed with deep pockets, and significant political pull.

One thing is for sure: you wouldn't ever want to dance a jig or a two-step with the beef lobby! (Coincidentally, when Kirstie Alley first heard the term "beef lobby" -- she thought it was a nickname for the waiting room at Overeaters Anonymous.)

Foot in Mouth Disease?

In 1998, Oprah Winfrey was sued by more than 100 Texas ranchers. Turns out, they weren't thrilled with a couple of television shows she had done regarding mad cow disease. They claimed that as a result of her shows, beef sales plummeted more than $10 million dollars.

After an explosive (and high-protein!) two-month trial -- one which ended up costing her millions of dollars -- Oprah was cleared of any wrongdoing. And although she had succeeded in vindicating herself in open court, she said afterward that taking on the beef industry was perhaps the worst thing she could ever have done...and that she would never do it again. Throughout the trial, she had been accused of being a liar, a publicity-hound, a mad cow, and a trouble maker, by, not just the cattle ranchers, but also their many allies and supporters. This was Texas, after all: the land of oil stains and cow farts.

This nightmarish, rodeo-from-the-depths-of-hell-like experience nearly led to Oprah to swear off all-things-Texas. For example, she couldn't even stomach watching the TV show *Three's Company* anymore; mainly because they kept mentioning "Ropers". ("Turn that shit off! Fucking hillbilly bumpkin redneck ropers...")

Objective onlookers, on the other hand, felt that it was entirely unfair the way that beef growers had branded her. (Get it? -- "branded"?) But nevertheless...many loyal Texans wanted to steer her wrong. Some attempted to jump on her back and ride her for a count of eight seconds. Several even tried to trip up her calf!

But Oprah is one of those blue-ribbon performers who stands apart from the crowd; usually over by a trough. A truly independent animal. She is often seen...but seldom herd. She's an award-winning breed who has no time for clowns. And if she has a cause that she feels passionate about, well, then, you can rest assured that not even wild horses could keep her away.

Her all-time favorite musical duo is Hall & Oates. Well, that's not entirely true. She was never really crazy about Hall...but she loves her oats.

Comfort Foods

A donut hemorrhoid cushion.
Fruit of the Loom underwear.
These are both very comfortable.

Hot Food in the Summertime

The Dog Days of summer will soon be howling yet again. "Dog Days" are the hottest and most humid days of the year, occurring between July and September. That's when the brightest star in the sky, Sirius (the Dog Star), becomes visible. "Dog Days" does *not* mean that there are lots more dogs on the loose -- which would thereby make it harder to keep our shoes clean. Otherwise, they would be called the "Shoes Days" of summer.

The ancient Romans and Greeks joked that the blazing heat would drive dogs mad. That's what led to the star being named "Sirius," which means "scorching" or "burning" in ancient Greek.

Keeping cool during the Dog Days can be challenging -- especially if you don't have air conditioning at home, at work, or in the car. Even dogs themselves find it difficult to keep a leg up on the heat. Maybe that's the real reason why they love being around fire hydrants so much: they know there is precious relief hiding in there, but they just can't figure out a way to get at it. ("They invented a Monkey Wrench...why the hell couldn't they invent a Doggie Wrench?")

There are always methods available to lower the temperature a little. All you have to do is use your imagination.

Here are a few suggestions.

Walk through restaurants; sit in front of people who are blowing on their food

Also a great way to meet new people! Of course, some of these new people might be similarly inclined to break a metal serving tray over your hot, sweaty head.

That is why it is generally a good idea to ask first *before* you sit down to join the table.

Next, you must consider proper decorum. You will find that this is best achieved by everyone sitting in a tight circle, while simultaneously blowing on the person to their immediate right. This way, the breeze is spread around equitably, and nobody is left out of the loop. Only don't blow too hard -- you might start a tornado. It's sort of like a séance. Except this one makes your hair move. Oh, and don't blow with your mouth full. You could take an eye out.

Throw yourself off the roof; enjoy pleasant breeze on the way down

As you may have guessed, the trick here is to survive the fall. Try to pick a landing surface that isn't overly intimidating. Whether jumping on to grass, gravel, or concrete -- placing a couple of mattresses at the bottom is always a good idea. You can always move up to higher roofs once your confidence level (not to mention your Health Care coverage) increases.

If a cop asks you what in tar-nation you think you are doing up there, just tell him you are a member of a Swinging Shingles Club.

Push your workplace to replace "Casual Fridays" with "Underwear Fridays"

Needless to say, this trend isn't to all tastes -- in light of how some people like to sit facing you with their legs spread wide apart. Especially hairy, fat guys.

Switch to energy-efficient/low-heat light bulbs

But first...stick your tongue in the socket. You'll be amazed how much cooler you feel by comparison once you remove it.

Throw yourself in the lake; train your dog to retrieve you

Save that fetch stick for a pleasant evening campfire instead.

Attach miniature battery-powered fans to your partner's nipple-rings

This method is ideal for both guys and girls.

For Guys: Remove your shirt. Simply snap on the fans (one per nipple ring). Relax into your favorite chair. Lean your head gently back into your folded arms. Then revel in all of the attention that the spinning propellers and happy whiz-whiz sounds are sure to generate!

Now it's up to the sweating masses to use the gift that you have provided them wisely and efficiently. Many will attempt to crowd around you in an effort to receive a wisp of collateral breeze. Oh, and try not to let the fact that you look absolutely ridiculous bother you too much.

One thing is for certain: you have just given the term "going for a whiz" a refreshingly new twist on hot summer days!

For Girls: Girls installing these devices are warned to keep the horsepower to an absolute minimum. Due to the laws of natural aerodynamics, they may be inclined to take off, and, in some cases, have actually been known to achieve full flight. But provided the necessary caution has been observed, your partner can then enjoy the resulting breeze by gently passing their face in front of your spinning breasts...er, I mean, fans. For obvious safety reasons, plastic propellers are preferable to metal ones.

After all, you are trying to keep each other cool out there -- not splice off somebody's nose.

Have a friend take you for a pleasant drive; mount yourself on the hood

Almost sounds like the premise for a Beach Boys song, doesn't it? Had this been an option back in the 1960's, we bet Brian Wilson would not have locked himself away in his bedroom the way he did. Some will attribute that behavior to possible mental issues, but we know better. It was undoubtedly an effort on his part to avoid the relentless California heat.

Sit in your cool wine cellar for extended periods

Many people like to hang sausages, salami, prosciutto, cheese, and ham in their wine cellar. If you stay down there for a substantial amount of time, the smell will eventually seep into your clothes. So, once you've emerged...don't be surprised if you wind up being followed around by a pack of dogs wherever you go.

Eat lots of ice cream

The co-founder of Baskin-Robbins, Winnipeg-born Irvine Robbins, died on Monday, May 5, 2008. He was 90 years old. The news came as quite a scoop, because everyone thought he would die on a Sundae. "He wanted to have his body frozen...but then he began to waffle," said his wife, who definitely wasn't in Good Humor at the time.

Stock prices dipped and figures were fudged, but it's a Sherbet they'll recover.

Mr. Robbins and his partner Burt Baskin had started the company in 1945. They went on to make a mint: namely, Mint Chocolate Chip, Green Mint Stick, and Peppermint Fudge Ribbon.

Irvine Robbins was straw-buried in a Maple Banana casket beside a Pistachio Walnut tree. A 31 gun salute followed.

Stand in a bucket of cold water

Important Reminder: this always works better if you remove your socks and shoes first.

Soak a towel with water; wrap it around your neck

Make triple-sure it's a towel -- and not a boa constrictor which was just removed by Billy the Exterminator.

Attach sprinkler head to penis; drink lots of beer; wait

For optimum efficiency, make sure there are no bends, knots, or crinkles in your hose.

Go to a public swimming pool

I've always preferred my women on the shallow side.

Play strip poker

First we strip…then I poke 'er.

Food Olympics

For the most part, the Olympics are boring as hell. Lots of sizzle...precious little steak. If it were up to me, there would be some changes made.

What they need is a good fattening up. So I went in there and "foodified" the events so we could all relate to them a little more. I give you...the Food Olympics!

Summer Games

- In the new **Greco-Roman Wrestling**, the athletes will first be required to bulk up on illegal steroids. Then they must eat packaged Chinese noodles, and drink white wine as they grappa. I mean grapple. The event will now be called **Canseco-Ramen Riessling**.

- In the new **Triple Jump**, the athletes must make their leap while successfully holding on to an ice cream cone. Depending on the flavor they've chosen, the event will now be called the **Raspberry Ripple Jump**, the **Chocolate Peppermint Ripple Jump**, the **Peanut Butter Ripple Jump**, or the **Fudge Ripple Jump**. If you drop the cone, it's an automatic disqualification. However, if the ice cream flies out of the cone and you still manage to catch it in your mouth before you land, you're awarded full points. If it lands on your head...you're just an idiot.

- In the new **Pole Vault**, the athletes will use a long, flexible pole as they attempt to clear a high stack of bowls filled with their favirute piping-hot soup. Fittingly, the event will now be called the **Bowl Vault**. This event has been known to result in severe scalding -- so you'd better not knock any over. Contestants who shriek the loudest when scalded will receive a complimentary trip to the burn ward at the hospital of their choice.

- The new **Decathlon** is still probably the most grueling competition, as it involves conquering ten events over a two day period. However, the athletes are no longer permitted to gulp down endless cups of coffee for the chemical advantage it will gain them over their opponents. Therefore, the event will now be called the **Decaflon**. Only decaffeinated coffee will be permitted. Thorough urinalysis testing will be performed both before and after the race...so make sure you're not drinking from the same cup they had you piss in.

- In the old **400 Meter Hurdles**, the runners would have to clear ten hurdles that were evenly spaced around the track. The new event is similar...but will now be called the **400 Meter Turtles.** Only instead of jumping, you must now bend down to pick up and eat ten delicious, chocolaty Turtles along the way. You must stay in your lane; and eating someone else's Turtles is strictly forbidden. (The sheer chocolaty-appeal of this event has even spilled over to influence that granddaddy of all annual bicycle races: the **Tortoise de France**.)

- The **3,000 Meter Steeplechase** is also commonly referred to as the **Obstacle Course** -- where the athletes are required to jump over and clear four barriers, plus a water jump. But instead of an **Obstacle Course**...the new event will now feature a **Popsicle Course**. The water jump will be replaced by a shallow pit containing 25 Popsicles and a counter top. You must split the Popsicles perfectly in half on the edge of the countertop. If any of the Popsicles breaks into more than two even pieces, you must stay behind and build a house made of Popsicle sticks before you can proceed with the race.

- Traditional techniques used in the **High Jump** include the **Fosbury Flop,** and the **Western Roll**. These techniques will now be replaced by the **Pillsbury Flop**, and the **Cinnamon Roll**. As the jumpers clear the bar, they must emit a giggling, "Hoo-Hoo!" sound for the jump to count...just like Poppin' Fresh would. One word of advice, though: do *not* poke the judge in the belly. He's liable to break open one of those stiff tubes of dough over your head. Oh, and one more thing: you can't take your turn until the timekeeper announces, "On your mark...get set... DOUGH!"

- The **Discus Throw** will now be replaced by the **Biscuit Throw**. This event dates back to Ancient Greece -- where the nude male contestants would compete in the hot sun with their freshly-baked biscuits fully exposed. It has also been commonly referred to as the **Discus Toss.** Hence, the expression **"Tossing Your Cookies"** has never been more apt. The name, "Discus," was shortened down from its original, "Discuss". But people couldn't see what the big deal was...and got tired of talking about it. ("Discuss? Discuss what?! That naked guy over there just threw something. What are we supposed to discuss?")

- The **Hammer Throw** will now be replaced by the **Hamburger Throw**. Originally, the athlete would toss a metal ball attached to a wire and a handle, while he spun around three or four times to pick up momentum. But then along came David Hasselhoff. Now, the athlete will spin around with a paper bag containing half a burger, while he vomits three or four times.

- **Archery** will now be replaced by **Starchery**. Instead of competitors shooting arrows at a target sporting a painted-on bull's eye...they will now shoot at potatoes, beans, and pasta: all foods rich in starch.

- **Badminton** will be modified by hitting sticks of gum over a net with a racket. It will now be called **Spearminton**.

- **Beach Volleyball** will now be replaced by **Peach Volleyball**. Everybody loves canned peaches. And, by golly, those girls have beautiful cans! Who the hell even cares about the score when they leave you feeling so warm and fuzzy! You'll notice that most of the girls play barefoot. Although, one person did come forward to suggest that they should wear some shoes: it was a Peach Cobbler.

- Without question, one of the most difficult maneuvers to perfect in **Diving** is the **Flying forward one-and-a-half Somersaults and Pike.** This will now be replaced by the **Flying forward one-and-a-half Tablesalt with Northern Pike**. Throughout the event, the swimming pool will be stocked with live fish. When the divers enter the water, they must catch one of the fish with their bare hands...which will then be cooked up and served.

- The term **"Track & Field"** will be replaced by **"Black & Peeled".** Whenever you're stuck with a bunch of over-ripened bananas, what do you do? You don't throw them in the garbage...you make a banana cake, right? Well, this way we can also use them instead of batons for passing around during relay races.

- Instead of a **Finish Line**...a **Spinach Line**!

- Instead of **Gold, Silver, and Bronze**... **Snap, Crackle, and Pop**!

- Instead of the **Pan Am Games**...the **Canned Ham Games**!

- Instead of **Parallel Bars...Caramel Bars**!

- Instead of **Adidas...Fajitas**!

- **Squash**...will retain its name.

Winter Games

- **Alpine Skiing** is basically just downhill skiing**.** It will now be replaced by **Alpo Skiing**. In this new event, the skier will be chased down the hill by a pack of hungry dogs, while smeared from head to toe with Alpo.

- **Curling** was traditionally played by tossing heavy, granite stones around a smooth ice surface as you would in shuffleboard. You needed big stones to play this game. The new event will now be called **Churning**; and it is played by bouncing metal containers filled with cream off of one another...until it turns into fresh, creamery butter.

- **Speed Skating** *used* to be a winter sport...but not any more. The event will now be called **Seed Skating;** and the ice skates have been replaced by roller blades. In **Seed Skating**, the skaters will circle a farmer's field during planting season...where they will sprinkle seeds as they go. Unfortunately, the winner cannot be determined until all the crops have finished growing. The one with the biggest fall harvest output wins.

The Food Pyramids

Ever wonder why the **Commonwealth Games** are never played in Egypt? It's because then they'd be known as the **Tutankhamunwealth Games**. Heavily-perspiring athletes wouldn't emit **Pheromones**...they'd emit **Pharoahmones**. And **Synchronized Diving**? It would be called **Sphynxronized Diving**.

Dangerous Barbecue Food

On May 23, 2008, 50 year-old Vladimir Turskov died near Moscow. Turskov and some friends had been outside barbecuing a traditional Russian shish kebab dish called "shashlik," when a raccoon walked by and bit Turskov on the hand. Turskov later died of rabies poisoning.

His wife suspected something might be wrong when she noticed her husband in the bathroom with a big face full of lather...and assumed he must be shaving.

It was then she realized that he didn't have any shaving cream.

Food and Larry King Live

Larry King began his career on radio back in the 60's (that's the *1960*'s). It was there that he perfected the style which he would eventually bring to his popular cable television show -- and which many other hosts would come to adopt as a template.

"Welcome to Larry King Live. We're here for the entire hour, and we're going to take your calls! Let's open up the phone lines. Pittsburgh, you're on the air......Go ahead, Pittsburgh......Are you there, Pittsburgh?......I'M FINE, WHAT'S YOU'RE QUESTION, PITTSBURGH?!!"

Larry King puts the eruption back in "interruption".

LARRY: What's your favorite color? Let me guess... beige?

GUEST: Well, Larry, beige is nice, but I've really always been partial to purp-

LARRY: Do you like soup?

GUEST: Soup is nice, yes, I like soup. But I prefer a nice thick cheeseburg-

LARRY: How's your wife doing? Is your wife alright?

GUEST: My wife's fine, Larry. She's been receiving therapy for her hip replacement and it's been a tough year all around, especially in light of the recent accidental death of our beloved pet German Shep-

LARRY: Have you ever been to Disneyland? It's kind of fun, eh? Lots of rides!

GUEST: I haven't been there for a while, but I remember it being rather expens-

LARRY: Cuyahoga Falls, Ohio, you're on the air......Go ahead, Cuyahoga Falls......Are you there, Cuyahoga Falls?......I'M FINE, WHAT'S YOUR QUESTION, CUYAHOGA FALLS?!!

A selection of some of the world's top forensic pathologists studied images of Larry's desiccated, lifeless, terrifying, cobra-like features on CNN, and concluded that there is precious little difference between Larry King Live... and Larry King Dead. Many of them still experience haunting nightmares to this very day. Several went blind. (Actually, to say they went blind is an understatement, and only partially accurate. The full truth is infinitely more grisly: their eyeballs literally ran screaming from their heads! The eyeballs were last seen on Eye-95...outrunning cars.) Three pathologists attempted suicide. Sorry, it was eight.

The goofy suspenders? They're not just for show, either. They're what are holding his rotted corpse together. We'll miss you, Larry.

"Tornado Hits Pig Farm: Inflation Expected"

Meat prices were going through the roof.
Sausages were soaring.
Pork chops were literally flying off the shelves.
And bacon is still spiraling out of control.

Food in Presidential Cars

In 1789, George Washington became the first President of the United States. 222 years and 43 Presidents later, there remains one and *only* one car that was ever named after a President. The Lincoln. The Lincoln got me thinkin'.

(For the record, the Ford Motor Company was not named after Gerald Ford. *Although*...Gerald's penchant for tripping over his feet and landing in a twisted heap did very nearly result in Ford naming a famous car after him. Not the "Edsel" -- the "Pretzel".)

In fact, there were prototype models named after several different Presidents.

Theodore Roosevelt (President 1901-1909)

Favorite Foods
Breakfast: Hard-boiled eggs, rolls, coffee, milk
Lunch: Bread, leftovers, crackers, milk, cantaloupe, tea
Dinner: Fried chicken, steak, hominy, milk

The "Teddy" was a veritable one-man death squad. This "Great White Hunter" was responsible for shooting and killing thousands of wild animals across the globe. In fact, the original stuffed "Teddy Bear" got its name in 1903 from one of Teddy's many hunting excursions. Accompanied by experienced Trackers, Land Rovers, and Cherokees, "Teddy" would go about shooting pretty near anything that moved. He shot Jaguars, Pumas, Impalas, Cheetahs, Rabbits, Lynxes, Bison, Broncos, Foxes, Gazelles, Rams, Wildcats, Larks, Mustangs, Road Runners,

Sables, Vipers, Sunbirds, Skyhawks, Falcons, Bobcats, Grizzlies, and Kodiaks...especially ones that were Chargers.

Herbert Hoover (President 1929-1933)

Favorite Foods
Breakfast: Eggs, griddle cakes, fried cornmeal mush,
Lunch: Virginia Ham, corn soup, cream of potato soup, cherries
Dinner: Lobster, gumbo, roast lamb, apple pie

The famous line, "a chicken in every pot and two cars in every garage" is commonly attributed to Herbert Hoover...but that's a Lada bunk. In reality, he never said it. It is remarkable how prophetic the quote turned out to be, however, being that The Great Depression occurred under his watch. I say prophetic because when it came to the economy...Hoover was a chicken...and the country went to pot.

Speaking of two cars in every garage, the Depression was something which the "Hoover" was never able to Dodge; and he wound up afraid of his own Shadow.

John Kennedy (President 1961-1963)

Favorite Foods
Breakfast: Poached eggs on toast, broiled bacon, marmalade, milk, orange juice, coffee
Lunch: Soup (New England Fish Chowder), grilled cheese sandwich, fruit
Dinner: Lamb chops, steak, baked chicken and turkey, mashed potatoes, seafood, beans

The "JFK" was taken out of circulation due to a blown head gasket. He resembled a Coupe de Ville...but was more of a Coup d'état.

Lyndon Johnson (President 1963-1969)

Favorite Foods
Breakfast: Chipped beef with cream, tea
Lunch: Beef stroganoff, deer sausage, hot biscuits
Dinner: Steak, hash, chow mein, chop suey, seafood, spinach

The "LBJ" did his utmost to drive the "JFK" off the road so that he could Escalade the war in Vietnam.

Robert Kennedy (Attorney General 1961-1964, Presidential Hopeful 1968)

In 1968 in Los Angeles the "RFK" was caught in heavy traffic -- where he got dented three times from behind at point-blank range. However, the car that got blamed for the damage -- the "Sirhan" -- was at no time ever parked behind RFK. He had been in front of him the entire time. This was no mere fender-bender. That's why eyewitnesses at the crash scene were stunned when the collision was ultimately blamed on Sirhan, for they felt that the official decision had been very self-swerving.

Robert owned many cars...but he died in an Ambassador.

Richard Nixon (President 1969-1974)

Favorite Foods
Breakfast: Fresh fruit, wheat germ, coffee
Lunch: Meatloaf, seafood salad
Dinner: Corn beef, cabbage, spaghetti and meatballs, lasagna, steak, cottage cheese

The "Nixon" doubled as the perfect taxi cab. Everyone hailed him as "Checkers". But his Cavalier attitude over Watergate earned him a Citation, causing his political career to go up in flames: it was a six-alarm Blazer.

Jimmy Carter (President 1977-1981)

Favorite Foods
Breakfast: Ham, scrambled eggs, buttered toast, fruit, orange juice, corn bread, coffee
Lunch: Soup/stew, sandwich
Dinner: Southern fried chicken, pork chops, squash, zucchini, beans, tomato, eggplant

The "Carter" ran on peanut oil. Unfortunately, he wasn't able to pick up the Tempo and Dart around the Iran Hostage crisis very effectively...so he wound up a Diplomat. Being a good ole country boy from Georgia, the radio worked, alright, but it only played one song -- "Take This Job and Chevette". I mean shove it.

Ronald Reagan (President 1981-1989)

Favorite Foods
Breakfast: Bran cereal, skim milk, whole wheat toast, eggs, fruit, decaffeinated coffee
Lunch: Macaroni and cheese, soup (minestrone, lentil, bean, Scotch broth), bread, fruit
Dinner: Roast beef hash, chicken, steak, chili, beef and kidney pie, Yorkshire pudding

The "Reagan" would forget where he was going, and then suddenly fall asleep at the wheel. And then, your wife would have to tell him what to do next. He used a "trickle-down" carburetor which leaked continuously and caused a huge mess. The "Reagan" continues to be the car of choice among the wealthy, privileged elite. That's because he succeeded in lowering their income-tax rates from 70% down to 28%.

Bill Clinton (President 1993-2001)

Favorite Foods
Breakfast: Cinnamon rolls, donuts, Egg McMuffin
Lunch: Cheeseburgers, chicken enchiladas, biscuits

Dinner: Barbecue, pizza, baked beans, tacos, sweet potatoes, cream pie

The "Clinton" really got around! But you had to keep him locked up in the garage or he would get himself into trouble by constantly exposing himself to some of the uglier models on the road. But for all his imperfections, the Clinton was a smooth ride who could easily navigate 3-way intersections. He always dreamed of having the freedom to take an Escort out for a spin; he enjoyed a good Hummer; and he really loved his Cougars. A hedonist while in University, he could often be found in the Lotus position.

Oh, and Monica? Her belly button wasn't an innie... it was an Audi.

Ross Perot (Presidential Candidate)

In 1992 the "Perot" came from out of nowhere and gained enough voter support to cause the powers-that-be in the Democratic and Republican establishment to become *mighty* nervous. This would be the first occasion in modern times that the two-party monopoly would be seriously threatened with defeat. Unfortunately, Ross couldn't maintain his Focus...and dropped out of the race. To this day he has never really provided a thorough explanation about his sudden resignation -- other than his daughter's wedding Fiesta was to be somehow "sabotaged".

Something sure scared him off, that's for sure. Was it a Gremlin? A Phantom? A Laser? A Meteor? An Avalanche? A Cyclone? A Firefly? An anal Probe?

George W. Bush (President 2001-2009)

Favorite Foods
Breakfast: Biscuits
Lunch: BLT/grilled cheese/peanut butter sandwiches, soup, chicken pot pie, burgers
Dinner: Mexican, pizza

A "W" will go out of his way to bankrupt you, so you're wise to keep your hand on your wallet at all times (now you Fiat...now you don't). Also, you should keep a steady eye on the road, for he has a bad habit of going to the wrong country to fulfill his gluttonous oil needs.

As we all know, George W. Bush likes to tell people how much he loves reading the Bible. Unfortunately, he spells it "Bibull". And George really puts the bull back in "Bibull"!

The following two quotes may well be among his favorites.

1. *"Christ our passover is sacrificed for us: Therefore let us keep the feast, not with the old leaven, neither with the leaven of malice and wickedness; but with the unleavened bread of sincerity and truth."*
1 Corinthians, 5. 7

Wow, that's a lot of "leavens". Practically eleven leavens. Take all the time you need to contemplate that quote, Georgie. What you need is a secure place that offers you plenty of time for solitary confinement. I mean reflection. Allow me to suggest a location that is in keeping with the true spirit of that quote: namely, Leavenworth.

2. *"If the trumpet give an uncertain sound, who shall prepare himself to the battle?"*
1 Corinthians, 14. 8

This passage inspired George to change the sound of his car horn to one that sounded more like the confident battle cry of an invading army. After all, this is something that is right up George's alley.

What these two quotes have in common is that they are both taken from Corinthians in the New Testament. That's why it should come as no surprise that the "W" was upholstered in fine, Corinthian leather.

But the "W" didn't stop there! It also featured a color-coded advisory system designed for preventive care. Red meant a SEVERE risk of rust attacks. Orange meant a HIGH risk of rust attacks. Yellow meant an ELEVATED risk of rust attacks. Blue meant a GUARDED risk of rust attacks. And green meant a LOW risk of rust attacks.

But this system was soon dropped when it became clear to people that it was nothing but a scare tactic designed to keep them in fear of an invisible bogey-man. In this case -- the terrorizing effects of rust.

Dick Cheney (Vice-President 2001-2009)

Favorite Foods
Breakfast: Small children (lightly toasted), crushed glass, a large goblet of fresh blood
Lunch: Tortured nuns, innocent virgin pieces, Scooter Libby's Beans, Blackwater
Dinner: Rats, scorpions, flies, bats, locusts, Waterboard Salad

"W's" disastrous and ill-fated spin-off -- the "Cheney" -- comes only in either mini or luxury sizes. That's because Cheney doesn't believe in middle classes.

After Cheney committed the traitorous act of outing a CIA agent out of retribution for her husband, Joseph Wilson, (who could definitively prove that Cheney's reasons for invading Iraq were totally bogus), there was talk of a new car being designed in his image. It was to be cold, slithery, low to the ground, and based on a Cutlass Supreme -- the "Gutless Supreme". Instead, they opted for a name that was more reflective of his complete lack of any trace of a heart whatsoever. Similar to the "Pacer" -- the "Pacemaker".

Barack Obama (President 2009-)

Favorite Foods
Breakfast: Eggs, bacon, potatoes, wheat toast, oatmeal, grits, fruit
Lunch: Chili, cheeseburgers, sandwiches
Dinner: Seafood, Mexican, Italian, broccoli

The "Obama" was available only in black...but he didn't use gas. He ran on Hope and Change. A Republican would never, ever, *ever* own an Obama -- because they absolutely refuse to admit that he's American-made. If a Republican ever did buy an Obama, it would be for one simple reason: because Republicans will forever have fond memories of owning something black that used to work on their cotton plantations.

During the election campaign of 2008, the Obama was pitted against a fading Challenger; an aging Maverick jalopy who was the epitome of an Oldsmobile. He was just plain Olds. Even though the Maverick never stood a chance, and was eventually left broken down and abandoned by the side of the road, he put up a Valiant effort. Many insiders believe the Maverick lost the race because of his allegiance to a bimbo nut-bucket who drove around in a Yukon.

Food in Movie Theaters

Going to the movie theater can be an exciting and rewarding experience. Not all films turn out to be quite worth the price of admission, however -- a fact we usually don't discover until we've already bought a ticket and planted our eager butts down into a seat. At that point, not even an extra-large box of delicious popcorn smothered with the finest high quality artificial golden topping butter substitute will lessen that crushing sense of disappointment...and of feeling ripped off.

With that in mind, what if we updated the Movie Ratings system to better reflect this all-too-frequent reality? This way, the cinema-going public could more accurately gauge what to expect going in. As it currently stands, movie ratings are simply not designed to determine whether a film is "good" or "bad," or to approve or disapprove of a film, but merely to act as a general guide to help parents decide which movies they want their children to see -- based on factors such as nudity, violence, mature themes, depicted drug use, or strong language.

It is fair to conclude that one's perception of a particular movie's merits is an entirely subjective exercise based on personal preferences. Something that appears "inspired, uplifting, and well-written" to one person, may seem "long-winded, tedious, and excruciating" to another. But surely we can get our ducks in a row to help weed out some obvious turkeys, here, no?

But first, here's a brief history of the process.

THE AUDIENCE IS GLISTENING

In 1930, the United States Motion Picture Production Code became the first governing body for ratings systems. This was revised in 1966, and again in

1968 - when the Motion Picture Association of America (MPAA) became the dominant entity. After much tinkering and efforts at re-classification along the way, the ratings were again modified in 1996 to reflect their present-day format.

The ratings used from 1996 to present are:

G: General Audiences
All ages admitted.

PG: Parental Guidance Suggested
Some material may not be suitable for children.

PG-13: Parents Strongly Cautioned
Some material may be inappropriate for children under 13.

R: Restricted
Under 17 requires accompanying parent or adult guardian.

NC-17:
No children under 17 admitted

Fair enough. It's a simple partnership, after all. Hollywood offers up its movies; and in exchange, we fork over our hard-earned money to watch them. Sounds like a marriage made in Heaven's Gate, right? But wait, don't we -- the frustrated consumers -- deserve more consumer-friendly movies? Why, of course we do, 007!

But what good will all of that do if they're camouflaged behind ratings that are misleading, superficial, or just plain inadequate? You need to read that little black label, Mabel. And so -- in the spirit of quid pro quo Vadis -- here is what the list of Movie Ratings *should* look like.

The New Movie Ratings

CF: Chick Flick

Buddy, you must have done something *real* bad to have agreed to this kind of torture.

MB: Monumentally Boring
Yawn With The Wind? Feel free to snore out loud.

US: Unbelievably Slow
You can stop tapping your watch…it's not broken.

WTL: Way Too Long
Just as neck-breaking as waiting on a doctor's appointment, but at least *there* you know you may be getting a prescription for some really cool drugs.

DB: Don't Bother
What were you thinking?

TAG-BYIJIC: Touch And Go – Bring Your iPod Just In Case
Music soothes the savage bomb.

SH-TM: Stay Home – Trust Me
Stay home. Trust me.

CUOYHCI: Catch Up On Your House Cleaning Instead
That basement isn't going to clean itself.

AMNM: A Measly Ninety Minutes
At ten bucks a ticket, that works out to…carry the one…more than eleven cents per minute. Unheard of in this economy!

MCINITO: Michael Caine Is Not In This One
Hey, give the old guy a break -- he can't be in *every* single movie ever made!

CEIITO-UHDSA: Clint Eastwood *Is* In This One – Unfortunately He Doesn't Shoot Anybody

Clint is always at his best when he has a score to settle. You feeling lucky, punk?

LOS-NP: Lots Of Splosions – No Plot
No brain cells were harmed during the making of this film.

DBAFD-OTWBASD: Don't Bring A First Date – Or There Won't Be A Second Date
Dinner and drinks is the smart option here, fella.

PB: Pretty Bad
Could be worse, you understand...but still pretty bad.

SOA-TTCRQ: Starts Out Alright – Turns To Crap Real Quick
This dud has only one or two decent scenes throughout. Usually, they're the ones you see in the trailer that tricked you into watching it in the first place.

TBTWSDLL: Too Bad The Writer's Strike Didn't Last Longer
I know it may sound hard to believe, but somebody actually *wrote* this mess! What's even more astounding is that somebody actually paid to have it produced.

EPTYOTCP: Encourage People To Yap On Their Cell Phones
Yes, this debacle is so bad that it has come to this. But don't be so skeptical. Some conversations between strangers can be rather fascinating, to the point where they may completely make up for the horrendous stiff of a movie you're stuck watching. And remember...if they insist on talking so loud, *technically* that means you are not snooping.

WDRET? WHDHUAF-BIDTIAT: What Does Roger Ebert Think? Well He's Definitely Holding Up A Finger – But I Don't Think It's A Thumb
Nuff said.

SSS-WYAOTGI?: Stars Steven Seagal – Were You Aware Of That Going In?
Do not walk but RUN to the nearest exit. There's still time.

MMGSIACOS: Matthew McConaughey Goes Shirtless In A Couple Of Scenes
Just a little heads-up for all you interested girls out there. Or guys.

WFTDVD: Wait For The DVD
Still risky watching it at home, but at least there you can quickly turn it off and salvage your night by doing something more worthwhile -- like re-washing the dishes...or re-reading yesterday's junk mail.

PHM – TMSTAMMIHHBIOHIOTHDTSASFWII – AHSCTSHSTMBSBTD - SHPIAOTBSBALCS – TFTIOADCBHAGSOR – IATPTHWATA – OTBFSTDBTI: Predictable Horror Movie – The Moron Suspects There's A Murderous Maniac In His House But Instead of Hightailing It Out Of There He Decides To Stay And Search For Whoever It Is – As He Slowly Continues The Search He Suspects There May Be Something Behind The Door - So He Pushes It Aside Only To Be Startled By A Loud Cat Screech – The Fact That It's Only A Damn Cat Brings Him A Great Sense Of Relief – It's At This Point That He Will Abruptly Turn Around – Only To Be Fatally Stabbed To Death By The Intruder
You'd think the same guy wrote every horror movie ever released since about 1978.

DDT – IWWMNGMADLTM - IHHDTIWMWKHBBFWEPBO – IWEHATT: Day Dream Time - I Wonder Why My Neighbor Gave Me A Dirty Look This Morning - I Hope He Doesn't Think It Was Me Who Knocked Over His Recyclables Box Filled With Empty Plastic Bottles - I Wasn't Even Home At The Time
It's amazing how your mind will wander during this clunker of a movie.

Wasn't that helpful? If you follow these new ratings to the letter, the only surprise you should be receiving at the movie theater will be in your box of Cracker Jack. Wait a second... do movie theaters even sell Cracker Jack? The surprises never end.

Booze

The story you are about to hear is true. The names have been changed to protect the Anisette.

Madame Butterfly is a lush opera. Madame Barfly is an opera about a lush. But where Madame Butterfly buckles under the anguish of unrequited love and impales herself on a dagger...Madame Barfly goes backstage with the Rolling Stones and impales herself on Mick Jagger.

A Short History (Just a little snort)

Alcohol has been with us in one form or another for tens of thousands of years. Everybody can remember when man first walked on the moon. But nobody knows when man first stumbled home in a drunken stupor.

Unfortunately, recorded history doesn't go back that far, so we'll never know for sure who first invented it and where. The best evidence points to the earliest civilizations which existed at the time -- namely, the Middle East, China, and India. (For those of you who guessed "Ireland," you should be ashamed of yourselves.)

The earliest spirits were likely made from berries or honey. This might explain why bears always appear to be smiling. It might also explain why Curious George was so curious during that camping trip back in College.

Winemaking began in the Middle East somewhere around 6,000 BC. Winemaking in Europe began about 1,000 years after that.

Beer and ale date all the way back to 6,000 BC in the Middle East (Iraq, Iran), and China.

Although the art of distillation originated in Iraq around 2,000 BC, it wasn't used for making alcohol at this time -- but rather, perfumes and colognes. (You would think all those New York City cab drivers would smell better?) It wasn't until the 14th Century that the Irish would first employ distillation in the making of whiskey. (For those of you who guessed "Ireland" earlier on, you're finally correct. Have a shooter. What's that -- you say you've already had five since the first guess?)

Vodka evolved in Russia, Eastern Europe, and Scandinavia in the 1300s.

Earlier rum-type drinks had existed for centuries, but they wouldn't be perfect until the 1600s in Caribbean colonies, like Barbados.

Most other alcoholic beverages (like Tequila, Brandy, Champagne, Gin, etc.) weren't invented until relatively recently -- from the Middle Ages up through the 16th, 17th, and 18th centuries.

In England during the Middle Ages, people were even permitted to pay their rent with beer. Although it is not known whether the terms "back rent" and "back wash" are in any way related.

During this period, Beer would be served up in pints (p's) and quarts (q's). Toward the end of the evening, an employee from the pub would yell at the patrons to "mind your p's and q's" as a reminder to not get too sloshed.

The traditional English "Yard" glass dates back to the 17th century. It is a narrow glass, a full yard long, which holds 2.5 pints of beer. Of course, one yard also equals 36 inches. A well-endowed male customer might have proposition a lady at the pub by saying: "Come over to my place sometime...I'll show you my *Scotland Yard*!"

Prohibition

In the early 20th Century, several countries around the world decided that the best way to combat the evil effects of that wicked, wicked alcohol was by controlling it in one way or another, or by banning it outright. This included Canada, The Soviet Union, Iceland, Norway, Hungary, and Finland. Most of the pressure was mounted by women's groups and religious organizations. But the most famous example, by far, was the United States, which remained officially "dry" from 1920-1933.

Prohibition was intended to ban the sale, manufacture, and transportation of alcohol for consumption. What were they thinking?

About the only thing Prohibition ever truly succeeded in accomplishing was making a lot of people honking rich. The American Mafia got rich (Al Capone alone earned $100 million dollars a year), as did the Canadian whiskey makers, Caribbean rum runners, and English gin distillers -- all of whom supplied the Capones,

Lucky Lucianos, Meyer Lanskys, and Bugs Morans's of the world with much of the finest booze available at the time. These products would discreetly find their way across the U.S.A, and directly into the mouths of thirsty and appreciative customers who were intent on taking the edge off.

The "Roaring Twenties" was an exciting era in America. This was the period when mass production would practically transform the country overnight, and launch it head-first into the modern age. To accommodate Henry Ford's hugely-successful Model T, newly paved roads and highways began to spring up everywhere, thereby connecting the country like never before. In addition, this was the period when such novelties as movies, radio, electricity, indoor plumbing, and the telephone would all become affordable and attainable by the average working person.

The term "bootlegging" originated from the way customers were required to literally conceal a bottle of alcohol in their boot as they enjoyed a drink at the local speakeasy. A "speakeasy" was so named because customers would be required to keep their voices down so as not to attract attention from the pesky authorities. On the positive side, this *was* the Depression, and all of that rampant "rum-running" resulted in thousands of employment opportunities for young and old alike, and would even inspire a cherished American song written in 1926: "Tiptoe Through the Juleps".

It was also during this period that "mixed drinks" first became widely popular. That's because much of the second-rate "bathtub liquor" in circulation tasted so vile that it needed to be mixed with some other beverage to help make it more palatable. Soda Water, Ginger Ale, Quinine, Tonic Water, and Cola all entered the mix.

Of course, plain old everyday water could also be used as a mix -- whether it came straight from the tap, or out of a well. In fact, if somebody asked, "is that well water?" -- a smart-ass bartender might reply, "Yes, it's very well, thank you". Speaking of wells, what did the Big Dipper say to the Little Dipper?

"You're looking a little pail."

Alcohol as Medicine

Alcohol had long been the ideal disinfectant for cuts, scrapes, bruises, and infections. It was cheap, and it was available. Before the invention of hospitals or anesthetics, a patient would be liquored up to the point of oblivion before potentially-painful surgery was performed. And if the booze didn't knock them out...you could always break the bottle over the person's head.

Alcohol Consumption by Country

Liters per capita

Liquor
1. (15.6) Luxembourg
2. (13.7) Ireland
3. (13.6) Hungary
4. (13.2) Moldova
5. (13.0) Czech Republic

Beer
1. (156.9) Czech Republic
2. (131.1) Ireland
3. (115.8) Germany
4. (109.9) Australia
5. (108.3) Austria

In case you're wondering how the high level of drinking in these countries translates into accidental car crashes, only Hungary and the Czech Republic rank in the Top 10.

In case you're wondering how the high level of drinking in these countries translates into life expectancy, here's how they rank out of a list of the Top 200.

#32 - Luxembourg
#29 - Ireland
#78 - Hungary
#118 - Moldova

#44 - Czech Republic
#23 - Germany
#5 – Australia
#16 - Austria

Not bad at all. And so, it appears that, other than Moldova and possibly Hungary, the majority don't seem to be too adversely affected by their heavy boozing. It has much more to do with the relative prosperity of the particular country involved, including the quality of health care it provides.

Marriage Vows for the Designated Driver

Did you ever notice how practically every guy you know who plans to attend any function which involves alcohol will inevitably rely on his wife to drive him there? This is perhaps especially true during the party-riddled Christmas Holiday season -- when police presence on the roads is ramped up like no other time during the year. For this reason alone, it pays to be cautious when traveling from Point A, to Point B, to Poinsettia.

How are you getting there, Bill? "Oh, my wife's driving me."

How about you, Bob? "My wife's driving me too."

Gary? "Wife."

Ahmed? "Same."

Ranjeep? "Ditto."

But what about the poor bastard who is single? Not every guy in this world can be lucky enough to marry a nice, reliable designated driver. Oops, I mean a wife that he loves.

Let's clear the air here and identify the 1,000 lb. Elvis in the room. Er...I mean elephant. Most guys don't get married for love. They get married because they know it'll bag them a private chauffeur. Hell, it beats taking the bus...and it's a hulluva lot cheaper than cab fare, too. ("Read my lips: No More Taxis!")

The least we can do is be honest about it. In fact, this practice is so widespread in our society that it should be reflected in our marriage vows, as well.

"Larry, do you take Anne to be your lawfully wedded Designated Driver? (He responds 'I do.') Do you promise to love and cherish her, and help her pay for any traffic tickets incurred while she drives you around the city in your drunken pursuits, and let her do all the talking if the cops ever pull you over, and never make a fuss when she offers you a stick of gum because your breath could peel paint, and install a functioning GPS, in sickness and in health, in two-door, sedan, wagon, or mini van, for richer or poorer, in automatic or standard, in front seat or back, in domestic or import, for better or for worse, and forsaking all others, hand your car keys only unto her, for so long as you both shall travel? (He responds 'I do'.) Do you together promise in the presence of your friends and family that you will at all times and in all circumstances and road conditions learn to brake effectively to prevent swerving, pull over to the shoulder if he needs to vomit, and conduct yourselves toward one another as Husband and Designated Driver? (Both respond 'I do'.) Do you together promise that you will love, cherish, and respect the rules of defensive driving and overall highway safety throughout the years? (Both respond 'We do.') Then, by the powers vested in me by the Department of Motor Vehicles, I now pronounce you Man and Designated Driver. Larry, you may kiss your driver."

At the conclusion of the ceremony, the priest and the groom clink their champagne-filled glasses together, accompanied by an enthusiastic "Cheers!" Then the brand new wife drives them to a bar, where the priest proceeds to...ahem...drink her husband under the table.

Alcohol-Related Myths

A "teetotaler" is someone who abstains from alcohol. It's not someone who drives carelessly and then totals his Model T.

A "Topless Club" is a place which features live female nudity. It's not a bar that's missing a roof.

Jesus never actually walked on water. What happened was that he and a bunch of drinking buddies went up to the cottage to get away for the weekend and toss back a few cold ones. He eventually sprinted down to the shore to take a much-needed, bladder-bursting leak into the lake. One exaggeration led to another...and a Biblical myth was born.

Jesus himself was quite irate at the distortion -- to the point where people would say to him, "Hey, Jesus -- why so cross?"

Open Bar

I named my twin boys "Martini" and "Rossi". Funny thing about those two little guys, though. Whenever I'd take them to the beach, they'd never play in the sand... always on the rocks.

When my wife first told me she was pregnant with twins, I began to sweat bullets. And as every drinker will tell you...nobody can sweat bullets like someone who is good and loaded.

Drink responsibly. Drink less. Besides, you know what they say about cowboys who drink too much, don't you? They often end up shooting blanks

----

A handsomely-crafted, well-stocked liquor cabinet is traditionally the centerpiece of any warm and inviting living room. Yet the very name itself -- "Cabinet" -- acts as a subtle reminder that we should leave our keys and take a taxi instead. Namely, if consuming alcohol, you shouldn't be driving anywhere...you should be "cabbin' it".

Booze at a Job Interview

Consider the crusty company president as he sits there sizing me up; eying me up and down in a tomblike-serious manner, as he reflects upon my potential value as an employee. Finally, after an intense and studied pause, he leans forward, plants his elbows on top of his antique oak desk, clasps his meat hooks firmly together, narrows his beady eyes, and says: "Alright, Frank, I've listened to you speak. Now, tell me...what can you bring to *our* company?"

This is it. It's all-or-nothing time. I slant my head askew: not unlike a hopelessly confused dog; desperate that anything remotely resembling an inspired retort would hopefully squeak-toy its way past my raised, floppy ear... and into my ample brain jelly. But, goddammit, that was one tough question: one which left me tied up in knots, helpless, on the ropes, and unable to move. Hey, who does this guy think he is, anyway -- Half-Nelson Rockefeller? Fuck him and the hearse he rode in on!

(Most people's brains are jam-packed with grey matter -- that all-important gelatinous goo which allows them to process complex information at lightning-fast speed. But mine just has a distinguished touch of grey at the temples...and a few streaks around the cowlick. Some men go prematurely grey; I went prematurely stupid.)

I decided to respond anyway. "Ummmmm..........my lunch?" (Employer drops his head to his chest.)

I respond a second time. Only *this* time displaying the type of exhilaration usually reserved for someone who has just possibly stumbled on to some profound, world-beating invention, and who now has to work extra hard to try and sell it. Like, say, the cure for baldness. Or a deodorant stick which has more than an eighth of an inch of actual deodorant in it -- even though the container itself is about five fricking inches tall. The rest is the damn turning mechanism.

"The *flu!*" (Employer begins to shake his head.)

By that point I sensed my future with this company was most likely over. So I did what anybody else who can take a hint that they are not wanted would do: I picked up my glass of wine and walked right out of that office.

Booze at Funerals

Here's the thing: funerals are way too somber. And sober. And the wake before the funeral is even worse. There, you're actually standing face-to-face with a real live dead person!

This begs the question. Where's the booze?

Unfortunately, most Funeral Parlors do not even qualify for a liquor license due to "sanitary" considerations. You'd think the reverse would be true. After all, can you think of a better place to kick back and pour yourself a stiff one?

Bars and Funeral Parlors have so much in common that their similarities should be celebrated...not cremated.

You could belly up to the bar...or just be plain belly up. You could be pining for a drink...or just lying in a pine box. You could be feeling no pain at last call...or just feeling no pain at last call.

On the other hand: "He has gone to a better place," may indeed mean the guy died; or it may just mean that he went to a nicer bar. And when I hear that someone has "shuffled off their mortal coil," it can only mean one thing: coat check. However, I don't think the term "passed on" should ever apply to people who cherished their booze while they were still alive. Like W.C. Fields, for example. He never passed on a drink in his life.

In May of 2008, an Illinois man had a custom-built coffin made up in the shape and colors of a Pabst Blue Ribbon beer can. He plans to be laid to rest in it whenever his time finally comes. But in the meantime...he uses it as a beer cooler for himself and his buddies.

Hey, who wouldn't want to be buried with a nice, cold one? And nothing goes down smoother! But if I were him, I'd have the coffin laid to rest in an upright position: nobody likes flat beer. In addition, each coffin comes with an expiration date; because why should your beer expire just because your loved one has? Keep in mind, people, that the coffin can be used only once, so please...no empties!

Do you come from a big family? You're in luck! Family plots are available in 6-packs, 12's, and 24's. We can design our coffins to fit people of any size; but we specialize in tall boys, half-pints, longnecks, and stubbies.

Participating locations don't use formaldehyde to treat the corpses, either. We use a blend of vodka and tequila. We also offer an open bar in the chapel to help you through your grief...and a bouncer, to help you through the back door if you get too smashed. Just look for our sign out front: "We put the "bombed" back in embalmed!"

Eating with the Oscars (Or, Absence Makes the Henry Fonda)

What stands 13.5 inches tall and weighs about 8.5 lbs? If you guessed Jon Stewart... you're not far off! Actually, it's the one and only Academy Award: better known as an "Oscar".

The Oscars have long held a special place in the hearts and minds (and stomachs!) of film lovers everywhere. It's the one night of the year when Hollywood's biggest and brightest stars assemble for a night of mutual recognition and congratulation. It's also a night when many cinema devotees host their very own Oscar-night house parties.

But what would you serve your guests at such a party? Well, with a little ingenuity and planning, you can offer your guests a spread that itself might be worthy of an award. You needn't go to the time and expense of having it catered, and it would certainly be more original and infinitely more memorable than if you'd just passed around a couple of bags of chips.

Have you ever considered throwing your own Oscar bash?

There is no shortage of tasty movies, tangy actors, and mouth-watering film roles from which to draw your inspiration for possible menu ideas. Of course, some performers stand out among the rest.

The legendary Garlic Brando excelled in *On the Watermelon* (1954*), A Snack Bar Named Desire* (1951), *The Codfather* (1972), and *Last Mango in Paris* (1972). If you ever saw him towards the end of his career, you'd find it difficult to believe that he was ever a "starving" actor. He stood out in more ways than one.

Director Francis Ford Coppola is on record for saying that Brando was a very good listener. Francis wouldn't have to tell him the same thing three times. He wouldn't have to tell him four times. Just a Coppola times.

Similarly, the quirky Jack Pumpernickelson left people salivating with *One Flew Over the Couscous Nest* (1975), *Fava Easy Pieces* (1970), *Mallomars Attacks!* (1996), and *A Few Good Menus* (1992). These actors weren't afraid to leave their audiences wanting a second helping.

But they are not alone. Consider the following list of other notable films and film personalities. They've all left their mark on plenty an audience...and plenty a napkin as well. They might not all have won an Oscar, but you can rest assured that they are quite familiar with Oscar Mayer.

Are you hungry for a delicious film feast? Allow me to suggest some blockbuster favorites -- both pasta and present. After you're done, I encourage your feedback. Well, everybody except for Charlton Heston, that is. He has the right to remain Soylent.

Breakfast:
- *Unwaffle Entry* (1992)
- *Casper (the Friendly Toast)* (1995)
- *Teabiscuit* (2003)
- *The Cruller Purple* (1985)
- *True Grits* (1969)
- Porridge C. Scott (Actor, 1927-1999)

Cereal:
- *The Courtship of Shreddies Father* (1963)
- *Every Thing You Always Wanted to Know About Chex But Were Afraid to Ask* (1972)
- *Pebbles Without a Cause* (1955)
- *The Sound of Mueslix* (1965)
- *Mad Max Beyond Honeycomb* (1985)

Appetizers:
- *The Amityville Hors D'oeuvre* (1979)
- *Lox, Stock, and Two Smoking Bagels* (1998)
- *From Herring to Eternity* (1953)
- *The Last Temptation of Rice* (1988)
- *Big Truffle in Little China* (1986)
- *The Manchurian Cantaloupe* (1962)

Poultry:
- *Gone with the Wings* (1939)
- *To Grill a Mockingbird* (1962)
- *Bang the Drumstick Slowly* (1973)
- *Goosebusters* (1984)
- *The Mod Squab* (1999)
- *Legends of the Fowl* (1994)
- *Grouse on Haunted Hill* (1959)
- *Poultrygeist* (1982)

- *The Roast and Mr. Chicken* (1966)

Pork:
- *The Loin King* (1994)
- *Who's Afraid of Virginia Ham?* (1966)
- *The Sowshank Redemption* (1994)
- *Honey, I Shrunk the Ribs* (1989)
- *The Days of Swine and Roses* (1962)
- *Chitlin Chitlin Bang Bang* (1968)

Beef:
- *Burgers in the Rue Morgue* (1932)
- *Steaks on a Plane* (2006)
- *The Barbecue of Seville* (1944)
- *An American Meatloaf in London* (1981)
- *The Taming of the Stew* (1967)
- *To Sirloin with Love* (1967)
- *Braising Arizona* (1987)
- *The Oxtail Incident* (1943)
- Stockyard Channing (Actress, 1944--)

Seafood:
- *The Silence of the Clams* (1991)
- *Mr. Holland's Octopus* (starring Richard Dreyfish) (1995)
- *Dude, Where's My Char?* (2000)
- *The Oysterman Weekend* (1983)
- *Mrs. Troutfire* (1993)
- *The Flounder of the Baskervilles* (1954)
- *StarKist Troopers* (1997)
- *You Otter Be in Pictures* (1940)
- *Crappie Gilmour* (1996)
- *On Golden Prawn* (1981)
- *The Unsinkable Mollusk Brown* (1964)
- *Tell Them Walleye Boy Is Here* (1969)
- Joan Crawfish (Actress, 1904-1977)
- Mussels Crowe (Actor, 1964--)

Pasta:
- *Bring Me the Head of Fettucine Alfredo* (1974)

- *The Shells of St. Mary's* (1945)

Sausages:
- *Jurassic Pork* (1993)
- *Bangers and M*A*S*H* (1972)
- *My Left Footlong* (1989)
- *The Merchant of Venison* (2004)
- *Broiling for Columbine* (2002)

Soup:
- *20,000 Leeks Under the Sea* (1954)
- *Borscht by Northwest* (1959)
- *Plan 9 from Chowder Space* (1958)
- *Indiana Jones and the Last Crouton* (1989)
- *Dr. Seuss: How the Spinach Stole Christmas* (2000)
- *Erin Broccolivich* (2000)
- *The Simmer of '42* (1971)
- *Star Trek II: The Broth of Khan* (1982)

MUSICAL INTERLUDE

(You've no doubt heard of the "Theme From Shaft". But have you ever heard the "Theme From Kraft"?)

"Who's the cheap macaroni dinner
That's a sex machine to all the chicks?
KRAFT!
You're damn right.

Who is the brand
That is fresh and firm and never bland?
KRAFT!
Can you dig it?

Who's the cat that won't crap out
When there's melted cheese all about?
KRAFT!
Right On!"

- Sung by Isaac Hayes in *Shaft* (1971)

END OF MUSICAL INTERLUDE

Italian:
- Panzarotti McDowall (Actor, 1928-1998)
- Pizza O'Toole (Actor, 1932--)
- Risotto Preminger (Director, Actor, 1905-1986)
- Pannetone Curtis (Actor, 1925-2010)

Sandwiches:
- *Baloney and Clyde* (1967)
- *The Purple Rose of Gyros* (1985)
- *Salami Dearest* (1981)
- *The Blair Sandwich Project* (1999)
- *The Little Shop of Hoagies* (1960)
- *The Spam Who Knew Too Much* (1956)

Potluck:
- *Buffet the Vampire Slayer* (1992)

- *The Lunchbag of Notre Dame* (1939)
- *Two Meals For Sister Sara* (1970)
- *Harold & Kumar Go to White Casserole* (2004)
- *The Picnic Papers* (1952)
- *My Dinner with Entrée* (1981)
- Deli Savalas (Actor, 1922-1994)

Caviar:
- *Cat Beluga* (1965)
- *Sturgeon for Bobby Fischer* (1993)

Salad:
- *Lettuce From Iwo Jima* (2006)
- *The Red Cabbage of Courage* (1951)
- *Kid Salahad* (1962)
- *The Texas Coleslaw Massacre* (1974)
- Romaine Polanski (Director, 1933--)

Potatoes:
- *Romeo and Julienne* (1968)
- *Taters of the Lost Ark* (1981)
- *Lord of the Fries* (1963)
- *Mashers of the Universe* (1987)
- Potatum O'Neal (Actress, 1963--)

Vegetables:
- *Hush, Hush, Sweet Shallot* (1964)
- *Corn on the Fourth of July* (1989)
- *How to Stuff a Wild Zucchini* (1965)
- *The Bourne Ultomato* (2007)
- *Pat Carrot and Billy the Kid* (1973) (Basted on a true story!)
- *Parsnip and Old Lace* (1944)

Fruits:
- *Kiwi's Big Adventure* (1985)
- *Jason and the Coconuts* (1963)
- *Peaches from the Black Lagoon* (1954)
- *Papaya (The Sailor Man)* (1980)
- *Plantains, Trains, and Automobiles* (1987)

- *Conquest of the Pomegranate of the Apes* (1972)
- *Brother Can You Spare a Lime?* (1975)
- *The Reluctant Apricot* (1967)

Bread:
- *The Fabulous Bakery Boys* (starring Chef Bridges) (1989)
- *The Secret of My Successame* (1987)
- *Passion of the Crust* (2004)
- *Alice in Wonder Bread* (1951)
- *Breadator* (1987)

Spreads:
- *Me, Myself, and Margarine* (2000)
- *Oh Butter, Where Art Thou?* (2000)
- Nutella Lugosi (Actor, 1882-1956)

Cheese:
- *Carlito's Whey* (1993)
- *Close Encounters of the Curd Kind* (1977)
- *The Guns of Provolone* (1961)
- *Swiss Cheese Family Robinson* (1960)
- *La Dolce Velveeta* (1960)
- Feta Garbo (Actress, 1905-1990)

MUSICAL INTERLUDE

"You say Mickey Rooney, and I say Macaroni
You say Don Knotts, and I say Donuts
Mickey Rooney, Macaroni
Don Knotts, Donuts
Let's call the whole thing awful."

– Sung by Fred Astaire in *Shall We Dance* (1937)

END OF MUSICAL INTERLUDE

Condiments: ("My condiments to the chef!")
- *Dial 'M' for Mustard* (1954)
- *Rosemary's Gravy* (1968)

- *And Justice for Salsa* (1979) (Al puts the Pacino back in "Cappuccino"!)
- *Much Ado About Stuffing* (1993)
- *The Life and Heinz of Judge Roy Beans* (1972)
- *The Tartar They Fall* (1956)
- *Cinderelish* (1950)
- *The Best Little Horseradish in Texas* (1982)
- *Home for the Hollandaise* (1995)
- James Oil Jones (Actor, 1931--)
- Martin Balsamic (Actor, 1919-1996)
- Worcestershirley Temple (Actress, 1928--) (Singer of "On the Good Shrimp Lollipop"!)

Spices:
- *All That Jasmine* (1979)
- *The Oregano Trail* (1959)
- *A Man for all Seasonings* (1966)
- *The Land Before Thyme* (1988)
- *Clear and Present Ginger* (1994)
- *Star Trek V: The Fennel Frontier* (1989)
- *2001: A Spice Odyssey* (1968)
- Parsley Snipes (Actor, 1962--)
- Nutmeg Ryan (Actress, 1961--)

Dessert:
- *The Bundt for Red October* (1990)
- *The Crêpes of Wrath* (1940)
- *Rumball in the Bronx* (1995)
- *Romancing the Scone* (1984)
- *The Fudge on the River Kwai* (1957)
- *A Midsummer Ice Cream* (1999)
- *The Mousse That Roared* (1959)
- *A Nut Cake on Elm Street* (1984)
- *Tamale Baba and the Forty Thieves* (1944)
- *Mutiny on the Brownie* (1935)
- *Puddin' on the Ritz* (1930)
- *The Tell-Tale Tart* (1953)
- *Eyes of Laura Marzipan* (1978)
- Nutty Ebsen (Actor, 1908-2003)

Potato Chips:
- *8 Heads in a Ruffles Bag* (1997)
- *28 Lay's Later* (2002)

Chocolate
- *The Maltesers Falcon* (1941)
- *Looking for Mr. Wunderbar* (1977)
- *Around the Werther's in 80 Days* (1956)
- Aero Flynn (Actor, 1909-1959)

Crackers:
- *When Harry Met Saltine* (1989)

Donuts:
- *Glazed and Confused* (1993)
- *The Snows of Cinnamonjaro* (1952)

Pie:
- *There's Pumpkin About Mary* (1998)
- *Dracula Has Raisin From The Grave* (1968)

Shortening:
- *The Count of Monte Crisco* (1956)

Spirits:
- *Spumante Python and the Holy Grail* (1975)
- *Whiskey Business* (1983)
- *Invasion of the Bacardi Snatchers* (1956)
- *Support Your Local Smirnoff!* (1969)
- *The Absinthe Minded Professor* (1961)
- *Whatever Happened to Baby Duck?* (1962)
- *The Beer Hunter* (1978)

Beverages:
- *Fanta of the Opera* (1925)
- *Dr. Snapple and Mr. Hyde* (1931)
- *Juice Almighty* (2003)
- *National Lampoon's Citrus Vacation* (1989)
- *The Sprite of St. Louis* (1957)
- *Cola Miner's Daughter* (1980)

- Huey, Louie, and Mountain Dewey (Donald Duck's nephews, born 1937)

Coffee and Coffee Substitute:
- *The Sanka Clause* (1994)
- *Murder on the Orient Espresso* (1974)
- *The Postum Always Rings Twice* (1981)

MUSICAL INTERLUDE

"You must remember this,
A knish is just a knish, a pie is just a pie.
The fundamental things apply
As time goes bye-bye."

- Sung by Dooley Wilson in *Casablanca* (1942)

END OF MUSICAL INTERLUDE

Coffee Whitener:
- *Creamer vs. Creamer* (1979)

Tea:
- *Kiss Me Tetley* (1955)

Chewing Gum:
- *Dubble Bubble Indemnity* (1944)
- *Willie Wonka and the Chicklet Factory* (1971)
- *The Talented Mr. Wrigley* (1999)
- *Annie Get Your Gum* (1950)

Licorice:
- *Twizzler on the Roof* (1971)

Mouthwash:
- *The Scope of Greenwich Village* (1984)
- *Austin Powers: International Man of Listerine* (1997)

- Lavoris Karloff (Actor, 1887-1969)

Toothpaste:
- *Bill & Ted's Pepsodent Adventure* (1991)
- *How the Crest Was Won* (1962)

Antacid:
- *The Birdman of AlkaSeltzer* (1962)
- Katharine Heartburn (Actress, 1907-2003), and Dispenser Tracy (Actor, 1900-1967)

Headache Relief:
- *Four Weddings and a Tylenol* (1994)
- *My Concussion Vinny* (1992)
- Jennifer Anacin (Actress, 1969--)

Cold, Flu, and Sinus Medication:
- *Gesundheit, and Good Luck* (2005)

Tranquillizers:
- *Sedative Night Fever* (1977) (This mega-selling soundtrack features the Bee Gees singing, "Ah, ah, ah, ah, Sautéing Alive, Sautéing Alive".)
- *How Green Was My Valium* (1941)

Erectile Dysfunction Medication:
- *Cialis Doesn't Live Here Anymore* (1974)

Hemorrhoid Relief:
- Preparation Heche (Actress, 1969--)

Colon Cleansing Medication:
- *Angels With Dirty Feces* (1938)

Bleach:
- Clorox Leachman (Actress, 1926--)

Window Cleanser:
- *Inherit the Windex* (1960)

May I have the envelope, please? And the winner is...you! Let's do it again next year. You know where you can find me... in the *Fridges of Madison County.*

The Beatles: Food On The Hill

A Beatles-themed restaurant? The Beatles still remain heavyweights of the music business some 40 years after their demise. After all, they provided the world with countless tasty melodies after cutting their chops in Liverpool and Hamburg. Their records and films were a feast for the senses and they really knew how to set the table with their delicious harmonies.

From the very first time we heard them sing, it was obvious to everyone how devoted they were to helping out around the kitchen. ("All My Oven, I Will Give To You...All My Oven, Darling I'll Be True.")

By 1966, the hectic pace of years of constant touring finally reached a boiling point and the band decided to concentrate on recording; it was here that they would really begin to heat things up.

Unlike those of "mortal" artists, Beatles fans tend to be of a different vintage Altogether Now. Theirs is a more discerning palate, resulting in a hunger for quality, good taste, innovation, and style. They consist of connoisseurs, restaurateurs, raconteurs, and Magical Mystery Tours. They can sense when something is golden; and that's why it's a virtual cinch that a Beatles-themed restaurant would amount to nothing less than another groundbreaking #1 Hit for the lads.

By comparison, the "Elvis Presley's Memphis Club Restaurant" lasted a scant six years, beginning in 1997. One can't help but wonder if the menu included "Deep-Fried Pelvis". It's a most unappetizing prospect, to be sure; for, what good would an Elvis menu be which didn't feature "Kielbasa Nova Baby," "Kissin' Croissants," or "Rock-A-Hula Baby Clams"? In the end, people took a queue from the movie, *Stay Away Joe,* and...well, stayed away, Joe.

It was a total *Spinout,* you might say. The combination of high lease rates plus low customer turnouts spelled *Double Trouble* for the establishment, resulting in the "King"-sized pantry doors being locked for good in 2003. You could say it was a case of "My Way" or the highway. ("And now, the end is near, and so I face the final gherkin.")

It's fair to say that things really began to spiral downhill for Elvis after his spectacular 1973 satellite concert, *Aloha From Havarti.* The title was merely a sad portent of what would lay ahead for the man who was once the brightest light at the buffet table. And you thought only his movies were cheesy? But that was hen and this is cow.

The Beatles would never have placed all of their career eggs in one basket like that. Not as a group, nor as solo artists. No, a Beatles-themed restaurant would feature only foods made from farm-fresh egg whites. No yolkos. Let's take a look at the menu, then, shall we?

Appetizers:
- Lovely Pita
- I Am The Eggplant, They Are The Eggplant
- Glass Onion Rings

Sandwiches:
- Sgt. Pepper's Lonely Hearts Club Sandwich
- No More Baloney Nights (Never Be Another)
- Take A Sad Salami And Make It Better

Soups:
- Happiness Is A Warm Gumbo
- Give Peas A Chance
- Magical Mystery De Jour
- Old Brown Stew
- Baby You're A Spinach Man
- She Came In Through The Mushroom Window
- Little Dumpling (It's Been A Long, Cold, Lonely, Winter)

- I Wanton You (She's So Heavy)

Side Dishes:
- Beans For The Benefit Of Mr. Kite
- Got To Get You Into My Rice
- Maharishi Mashed Potato Yogi
- I Coleslaw Her Standing There

Beef:
- Brisket To Ride
- Liver And Let Die
- I Want To Hold Your Hamburger
- Baby, You Can Drive My Tartare

Pork:
- Penny Loin
- Maxwell's Silver Ham
- Souvlaki Raccoon

Lamb:
- Juicy In The Fry With Diamonds
- Filet Tripper
- Yours Sincerely, Basting Away

Chicken:
- Oh! Garlic (Please Believe Me)
- Norwegian Wood-Stove (This Bird Is Cooked)
- Curry That Weight
- Wings At The Speed Of Sour

Duck:
- Quack In The U.S.S.R
- Vera, Duck, And Dave

Seafood:
- Mean Mr. Mussels
- Mishellfish
- What Would You Think If I Sang Out Of Tuna
- All Things Must Bass
- Rubber Sole

- When I Find Myself In Times Of Trouble, Calamari Comes To Me
- Father McKenzie, Writing The Words Of A Salmon That No One Will Hear
- We Shall Shrimp And Save
- The Lobster Winding Road

Pasta:
- Lady Lasagna (See How They Run?)
- I Wanna Be Your Manicotti
- Uncle Alfredo/Admiral Parsley
- Ravioli Shankar
- "Dig A Pony" Rigatoni

- Fusilli Love Songs

International Cuisine:
- While My Caviar Gently Weeps
- Instant Shawarma's Gonna Get You
- Here Comes The Tongue
- Cobra-Di, Cobra-Da
- The Squirrel That's Driving Me Mad Is Going Away
- Venison Mars (Are Alright Tonight)
- Kelp!

Cheese:
- Let It Brie
- It's Getting Cheddar All The Time
- Junior's Parm
- Gouda Day Sunshine
- Got A Good Reason, For Taking The Cheesy Way Out
- Cheese In Love With Me And I Feel Fine

Salads:
- Octopus's Garden Salad
- The Sea Of Greens
- P.S. I Love Fruit
- The Salad Of John And Yoko

Condiments:
- Everybody's Trying To Be My Gravy

Bread:
- Rolls Over Beethoven (with Sesame Mucho)
- The Bread Sullivan Show
- We're Gonna Have Some Bun Tonight
- Crust, You Know It Ain't Easy (You Know How Hard It Can Be)
- I Should Have Known Butter

Muffins:
- Bran On The Run

- Cruller Of Kintyre (served with A Taste Of Honey. Or, if you prefer it plain, just say "Honey Don't")
- For You Blueberry
- Muffin From Muffin Leaves Muffin (w/Billy Preston)

Donuts:
- Why Don't We Donut In The Road?
- Maybe I'm A Glazed

Desserts:
- Jell-O Submarine
- I Am The Walnuts
- Sundae's On The Phone To Mondae
- A Pretty Nurse Is Selling Pop-Tarts From A Tray
- Pie! Pie! Pie! (Served with Sweet Banana)

Breakfast Cereal:
- But Daniel Was Hot, He Drew First And Shot, And Rocky Collapsed In The Corn Flakes
- Four Thousand Bowls In Bran Flakes, Lancashire

Soft Drinks:
- Found My Coke, And Grabbed My Hat, Made The Bus, The Coke Was Flat

Tea:
- I'm Only Steeping (Note: All Tea is served with our home-made "Suddenly, I'm Not Half-And-Half I Used To Be" Cream...made fresh Yesterday)

Spirits:
- Twist And Stout
- Beer Prudence
- Imagine And Tonic

Wine:
- Cavern-et Sauvignon
- Rosé And Valerie

Champagne:
- Yesterday, All My Bubbles Seemed So Far Away

Throat Lozenges:
- Do You Want To Know A Sucrets?

Ahhh!...now, wasn't that delicious? So many timeless favorites—all of which hit the spot. To have to pick out only one would be like searching for a Beatle in a haystack. So, Come Together...and bring your appetite! The Hendersons will all be there.

Eat Your Way To The National Hockey League (or, Souvlaki Night In Canada)

NHL hockey players don't grow on trees (although many have been known to ride the pines). So, what then... are they hatched? Doubtful -- seeing as how the league has always proudly boasted having the fewest number of rotten eggs in all of pro sports. But what with the type of cabbage being doled out to players these days, it truly PAY$ for them to be devoted to their diets!

What are the main ingredients for success? Well, contrary to popular belief, "NHL" does not stand for "National Hibachi League". (Nor does it stand for "National Honkey League" -- despite the overwhelming majority of white players.) As a result of proper diet combined with a rigorous training regimen, a typical player will possess among the lowest body fat ratios of any professional athlete. Never before have players been in such tip-top condition; from before training camp even begins in mid-September, right through until the final Stanley Cup playoff game has been played in June.

By comparison, stars of yesteryear would use the exhibition schedule to literally play themselves into shape for the upcoming regular season.

A typical diet will include a carefully balanced blend of protein, fat, and carbohydrates. Pre-game meals are usually higher in carbs, ensuring an extra boost of much-needed fuel come game time. Junk foods and/or fried foods are generally discouraged as they tend to deplete much of the precious energy reserves which a player will rely on in "the crunch" -- or when being knocked head-first into the smorgas-boards.

Opportunity Knackwurst

Modern-day coaches love a player who is not afraid to go out and damage a few intestinal casings when the going gets rough. These players typically never complain, nor do they ever share their beefs with anyone. They never share their lamb or pork either.

This brings us to "Tough Guys". Tough Guys have long been mighty big fan favorites around the NHL. They fight, they grind, they intimidate, they punish, they protect. Every team carries at least one on its roster: a warrior who is capable of inflicting a veritable buffet of punishment, featuring all-you-can-eat left hooks.

Having said that, a player should use his toughness wisely and strategically. Nothing deflates a team more than a selfish, careless, or unnecessary penalty. Most teams have an "Elbows Macaroni" type of player who can't seem to control his arms very well. This player is obviously still working on his Kraft. (If hockey players truly think that they're so tough, then here's something I'd like to see them do. Never mind passing a puck... let's see them pass a kidney stone! Right there on the ice. In the middle of a shift!)

And while an assistant (or alternate) captain will proudly sport a large "A" on his jersey, you can easily pick out the player who has a serious drinking problem: he wears an "AA".

And now...here are some sensible food ideas served up by some of your favorite NHL stars.

Cereal:

- Count Chocula Plante, G (Montreal/NYR/St. Louis/Toronto/Boston, 434 wins, Vezina/Hart Trophy, 5 Stanley Cups)
- Frankenberry Sawchuk, G (Detroit/Boston/Toronto/LA/NYR, 447 wins, Calder/Vezina Trophy, 4 Stanley Cups)

- Shreddies Giacomin, G (NYR/Detroit, 289 wins, Vezina Trophy)
- The AlphaBitsburgh Penguins (Franchise, joined NHL 1967, 3 Stanley Cups)

Chicken:
- Thighs Domi, RW(Toronto/NYR/Winnipeg, 1,020 career games, 3,515 pim)
- Michel Poulet, LW (Quebec/Chicago, 548 goals/1,152 pts, Hockey Hall of Fame)
- Bruce "Finger Lickin'" Hood (Referee, 21 years/1,033 games)
- Lanny McNuggets, RW(Toronto/Calgary/Colorado, 500 goals/1,006 pts, 1 Stanley Cup)
- Cluck MacArthur, LW (Toronto/Buffalo/Atlanta)
- The Philadelphia Fryers (Franchise, joined NHL 1967, 2 Stanley Cups)

Pork:
- Shish Kebob Probert, LW (Detroit/Chicago, 935 career games, 3,300 pim)
- Teriyaki O'Reilly, RW (Boston, 891 career games, 2,095 pim)
- Wonton Stastny, LW (Quebec, 636 pts in 650 games, star forward of the 80's)
- Inge Hamstrung, LW (Toronto/St. Louis)

Beef:
- Perogy Vachon, G (Montreal/LA/Detroit/Boston, Vezina Trophy, 3 Stanley Cups)
- Rump Worsley, G (NYR/Montreal/Minnesota, 335 wins, Calder/Vezina Trophy, 4 Stanley Cups)
- Flank Mahovlich, LW (Toronto/Detroit/Montreal, 533 goals/1,103 pts, 6 Stanley Cups)
- Jocelyn T-Bone, G (Quebec/Colorado/Montreal/Chicago/Pittsburgh/Buffalo, 238 wins)

Grill:
- Zdeno Charbroil, D (NYI/Ottawa/Boston)

- Bill BarberQ, LW (Philadelphia, 420 goals, 2 Stanley Cups)

Seafood:
- Scallops Delvecchio, C (Detroit, 1,281 pts, 3 Stanley Cups)
- Cod Gilbert, RW (NYR, 1,021 points, Hockey Hall of Fame)
- Mike Calamari, LW (LA/Calgary/Montreal/2 others, forward)
- Clam Neely, RW (Vancouver/Boston, 395 goals, Hockey Hall of Fame)
- Filet Kessell, RW (Boston/Toronto)

Sushi:
- Patrick Raw, G (Montreal/Colorado, 551 wins, Conn Smythe/Vezina Trophy, 4 Stanley Cups)
- Wasabi Orr, D (Boston/Chicago, 915 pts, Calder/Norris/Art Ross/ Hart/Conn Smythe Trophy, 2 Stanley Cups)

Pasta:
- Phil Espoziti, C (Chicago/Boston/NYR, 717 goals/1,590 pts, Art Ross/Hart Trophy, 2 Stanley Cups)
- Spaghetti Shack, LW (NYR/Toronto/Boston/LA/Buffalo/Pittsburgh/, 1,047 career games, 4 Stanley Cups)
- Jean Belivelbow, C (Montreal, 507goals/1,219 pts, 10 Stanley Cups)
- Scarios Lemieux, C (Pittsburgh, 690 goals/1,723 pts, Calder/Art Ross/Conn Smythe/Hart Trophy, 2 Stanley Cups)

Soup:
- Alexander Ovechchicken, LW (Washington, Calder/Hart/Art Ross/Rocket Richard Trophy)
- Beef Magnuson, D (Chicago, 589 games)

- Nikolai Khabibouillon, G (Winnipeg/Phoenix/Tampa/Chicago/Edmonton, 300 wins, 1 Stanley Cup)
- Pea Lafleur, RW (Montreal/NYR/Quebec, 560 goals/1,353 pts, Art Ross/Hart/Conn Smythe Trophy, 5 Stanley Cups)
- The Minestrone North Stars (Franchise, joined NHL 1967, folded 1993)

(For a tasty and nutritious alternative, simply assemble a variety of your favirute ingredients, throw them into a pot...and just let them Simmer, Charlie.)

Italian:

- Pizza Forsberg, C (Quebec/Colorado/Philadelphia/Nashville, Calder/Art Ross/Hart Trophy, 2 Stanley Cups)
- Cannoli Jokinen, C (LA/NYI/Florida/Phoenix/Calgary/NYR)
- Panettone Twist, LW (Quebec/St. Louis, 1,121 pim)
- Biscotti Bowman (Coach/GM, St. Louis/Montreal/Buffalo/Pittsburgh/Detroit, 1,248 wins, 9 Stanley Cups)
- Domino's Hasek, G (Chicago/Buffalo/Detroit/Ottawa, 389 wins, Vezina/Hart Trophy, 2 Stanley Cups)

Cold Cuts:

- Borje Salami, D (Toronto/Detroit, 787 pts, Hockey Hall of Fame)
- Scott Niederoscarmayer, D (New Jersey/Anaheim, Norris/Conn Smythe Trophy, 4 Stanley Cups)

(Note: Although Cold Cuts should be consumed in moderation due to their relatively high sodium/fat content, nobody could ever forget the heroic exploits of Borje Salami against Philadelphia in the 70's... and he knew a thing or two about being sandwiched!)

Bread:
- Ryan Getzloaf, C (Anaheim)
- Pita Mahovlich, LW (Detroit/Montreal/Pittsburgh, 773 pts, 4 Stanley Cups)
- Panino Ciccarelli, RW (Minnesota/Washington/Detroit/Tampa/Florida, 608 goals/1,200 pts, Hockey Hall of Fame)
- Whole Wheat Stemkowski, C (Toronto/Detroit/NYR/LA, 967 games, 1 Stanley Cup)

Condiments/Spreads:
- Dijon Phaneuf, D (Calgary/Toronto)
- Horseradishlav Tretiak, G (Russian Goaltending Legend, Hockey Hall of Fame)
- Pâté Lafontaine, C (NYI/Buffalo, 468 goals/1,013 points, Hockey Hall of Fame)
- Chutney Crosby, C (Pittsburgh, Art Ross/Hart Trophy, 1 Stanley Cup)
- Dill Perreault, C (Buffalo, 512 goals/1,326 points, Calder/Lady Byng Trophy)
- Cheez Whiz Maniago, G (Toronto/Montreal/NYR/Minnesota North Stars/Vancouver, Original Six goaltender)

Mexican:
- Burrito Luongo, G (NYI/Florida/Vancouver)

Dairy:
- Jaromir Yogurt, RW(Pittsburgh/Washington/NYR, 646 goals/1,599 pts, Art Ross/Hart Trophy, 2 Stanley Cups)

Cheese:
- Cracker Barrel Sittler, C (Toronto/Philadelphia/Detroit, 1,121 pts, Hockey Hall of Fame)

Nuts:

- Cashew Barnaby, RW (Buffalo/Pittsburgh/Tampa/NYR/Colorado/Chicago/Dallas, 2,562 pim)

Vegetables:

- Yvan Cornonthecobyer, RW (Montreal, 428 goals, Conn Smythe Trophy, 10 Stanley Cups)
- Carrot Nesterenko, RW (Toronto/Chicago, 1,219 games, 1 Stanley Cup)
- Veggie Leach, RW (Boston/California/Philadelphia/Detroit, Conn Smythe Trophy, 2 Stanley Cups)

Fruit:

- Stan Chiquita, C (Chicago, 541 goals/1,467 points, Art Ross/Hart/Lady Byng Trophy, 1 Stanley Cup)
- Plantain Gretzky, C (Edmonton/Los Angeles/St. Louis/NYR, 894 goals/2,857 pts, Hart/Lady Byng/Art Ross/Conn Smythe Trophy, 4 Stanley Cups)
- Raisin Bourque, D (Boston/Colorado, 410 goals/1,579 pts, 1 Stanley Cup)
- The Avocado Avalanche (Franchise, joined NHL 1995, 2 Stanley Cups)

Chocolate Bars:

- Paul Coffee Crisp, D Edmonton/Pittsburgh/LA/Detroit/Hartford/Philadelphia/Chicago/Carolina/Boston, 396 goals/1,531 pts, Norris Trophy, 4 Stanley Cups)
- Snickers Kypreos, LW (Washington/Hartford/NYR/Toronto, 1 Stanley Cup)
- Smarties McSorley, D (Pittsburgh/Edmonton/LA/NYR/San Jose/Boston, 3,381 penalty minutes, 2 Stanley Cups)

- Eat-More Larionov, C (Vancouver/SanJose/Detroit/Florida/NJ, 3 Stanley Cups)
- Ullman Joy, C (Detroit/Toronto, 490 goals/1,229 pts, Hockey Hall of Fame)
- Nazem Cadbury, C (Toronto)
- 3 Palmateers, G (Toronto/Washington)

Bubble Gum:
- Bazooka Rask, G (Boston)

Cheese Puffs:
- Tony Espocheetos, G (Montreal/Chicago, 423 wins, Calder/Vezina, 1 Stanley Cup)

Discount No-Brand Food Products:
- Generic Lindros, C (Philadelphia/NYR/Toronto/Dallas, 865 pts, Hart Trophy)

Fruit Juice:
- Rick VaiveAlive, RW (Vancouver/Toronto/Chicago/Buffalo, 441 goals)
- Henrik Sunkist, G (NYR)
- The Clamato Maple Leafs (Franchise, joined NHL 1917, 13 Stanley Cups)

Mineral Water:
- Jacques LaPerrier, D (Montreal, Calder/Norris Trophy, 5 Stanley Cups)

Beer:
- Steve Budweiserman, C (Detroit, 692 goals/1,755 pts, Conn Smythe Trophy, 3 Stanley Cups)
- Pale Ale Hawerchuk, C (Winnipeg/Buffalo/St. Louis/Philadelphia, 518 goals/1,409 pts, Hockey Hall of Fame)
- Drunken Keith, D (Chicago)
- Labatts Sundin, C (Quebec/Toronto/Vancouver, 564 goals/1,349 pts)

- Gary Sleeman, RW (Toronto/Calgary/Montreal/Vancouver, 1 Stanley Cup)
- The St. Louis Brews (Franchise, joined NHL 1967)

Pop:
- Carlo CocaColaiacovo, C (Toronto/St. Louis)

Wine:
- Chablis Carbonneau, C (Montreal/St. Louis/Dallas, 3 Stanley Cups)
- Rosé Theodore, G (Montreal/Colorado/Washington/Minnesota, Vezina/Hart Trophy)

Rum:
- Bacardi Turco, G (Dallas/Chicago, 240 wins)

Vermouth:
- Martini & Bossy, RW (NYI, 573 goals/1,126 pts, Calder/Conn Smythe/Lady Byng Trophy, 4 Stanley Cups, Hockey Hall of Fame))

(Note: Let us make a special toast to the legendary Conachers -- Charlie, Roy, and Lionel. They are the only three brothers who are in the Hockey Hall of Fame. They Came. They Saw. They Conachered.)

Nausea/Vomitting/Dizziness Medication:
- Gravol Demitra, C (Ottawa/St. Louis/LA/Minnesota/Vancouver)

Antidepressant:
- Tyler Prozac, C (Toronto)

Diapers:
- The Florida Pampers (Franchise, joined NHL 1993)

Poison:
- Punch Hemlock (Coach/GM, Toronto/Buffalo, 423 wins, 4 Stanley Cups)

"He Shoots, He Scores!" – Lobster Hewitt

Remember, eating wisely needn't break the bank -- an important consideration in light of the current economy. But no matter how healthy a player is, he cannot control attendance. Several NHL teams are currently in danger of folding or being relocated. This has forever been a source of intense heartburn, acid indigestion, and upset stomach for the league, dating back to when the Mylanta Flames moved to Calorie, Alberta in 1980.

In fact, I'd like to go on...but my computer was just repossessed by the Nashville Creditors. I mean Predators.

Speaking of unethical behavior, I hereby propose that the NHL award a new annual trophy to its most despicable character. Perhaps something along the lines of the Conn Smythe Trophy; like, say...the Ex-Con Eagleson Trophy?

the ex-con eagleson trophy

10772979R00117

Made in the USA
Charleston, SC
03 January 2012